GOING HOME

God's plan to bring man back into relationship with Him.

authorHOUSE®

GOING HOME

God's plan to bring man back into relationship with Him.

Dedicated to Jim Young, Instructor

White's Ferry Road School of Biblical Studies

New International Version

Compiled
By

William E. Bradley

AuthorHouse™
1663 Liberty Drive
Bloomington, IN 47403
www.authorhouse.com
Phone: 1-800-839-8640

Published by AuthorHouse   03/12/2013

ISBN: 978-1-4817-2102-8 (sc)
ISBN: 978-1-4817-2101-1 (e)

Library of Congress Control Number: 2013903708

This book is printed on acid-free paper.

INTRODUCTION

We must believe that the "God of Abraham, Isaac, and Jacob" is also the "God and Father of our Lord and Savior Jesus Christ," and that "they which are of faith, the same are the children of Abraham," These are among the most precious truths of revelation. They show us not only the faithfulness of our God, and greatness of our privileges, but also the marvelous wisdom of the plan of salvation, and its consistency through out the Bible.

Alfred Efershem

CONTENTS

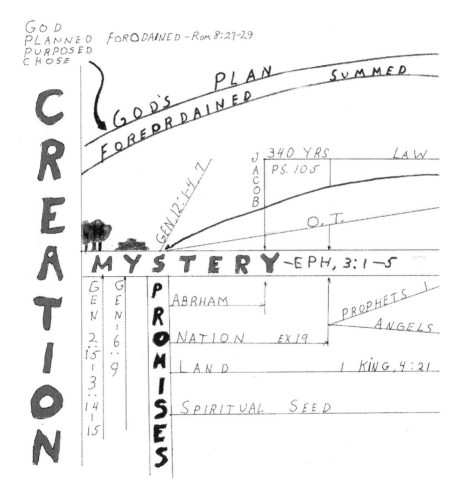

GOD
PLANNED   FORODAINED - ROM 8:27-29
PURPOSED
CHOSE

GOD'S   PLAN   SUMMED
FOREORDAINED

CREATION

GEN 12:1-4, 7

JACOB   340 YRS   LAW
        PS. 105

        O. T.

MYSTERY —EPH, 3:1~5

GEN 2:15-3:14-15   GEN 16:9   PROMISES

ABRHAM

NATION   EX 19   PROPHETS
                             ANGELS

LAND   1 KING, 4:21

SPIRITUAL   SEED

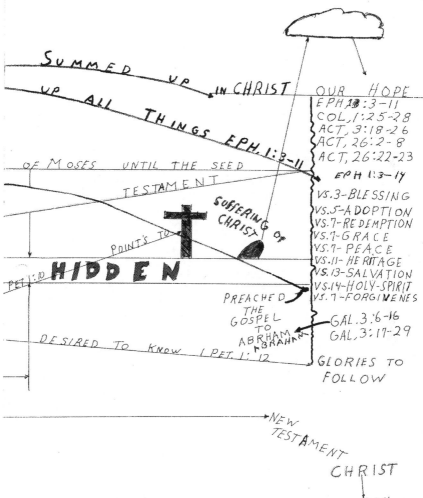

CHAPTER 1

The Beginning

A LIFE from DEATH and DESPAIR to LIFE and GLORY
God's plan to bring man back to Him.
A STUDY SO THAT THE WORLD MAY KNOW GOD

The ultimate object of our reading and study is not only knowledge, but also the understanding and experience of grace. The Scriptures are all full of Christ, and all were to point to Christ as our only Savior. It is not only the law, which is a schoolmaster to the coming of Christ, but all the examples, prophecies and predictions are the types, which are shadows of Christ. Even where persons are not, events may be types. The whole Old Testament history is full of Christ. If anyone failed to see in Isaac or in Joseph a personal type of Christ; he could not deny that the offering up of Isaac, or the selling of Joseph, and his making provision for the sustenance of his brethren, are typical of events in the history of Jesus Christ, so every event points to Christ and **God's scheme of redemption for man.** (BIBLE HISTORY OF THE OLD Testament by Alfred Edersheim William B. Eerdmans Publishing Co. Grand Rapids, Michigan. **(1)**

1. **The book of Genesis reveals God as the supreme Creator and Ruler of the universe and of His people. He can create whatever He desires to bring into the universe, and He does all His work by the use of the Word. (Logos) (John 1:1-5)**

A. **"And without faith it is impossible to please God, because anyone who comes to him must believe that he exists and that he rewards those who earnestly seek him." (Heb. 11:6)**

B. **The book of Genesis** is the period of time from the Creation to the settlement of the Israelites in Egypt.

C. **This** writer believes that Chapter 1 records the creation of all things and that scientific study shows that creation took millions of years to develop.

    (1. According to Bible historians, From the Garden of Eden in Chapter 2 through 11 records the first 2,000 years of history. During that time, three major events took place.

        a. The sin of Adam and Eve, ch. 3:1-13, note God's judgment in vss.14-19.
        b. Noah and the Ark and the great flood, ch. 8:1and ff.
        c. The building of the Tower of Babel; ch. 11:9.

2. **CHAPTER 12-50 OF GENESIS COVERS ABOUT 300 YEARS, CENTERING ON (4) four MEN.**

    a. **Abraham**. (2166-1991 B.C.)
    b. Entered Canaan at age 75 (Gen. 12:4). Death at age 175 (25:5).
    c. **Isaac born,** (2066 B.C.-1886 B.C) Abraham was 100 (21:5),
    d. **Jacob**.(2006-1859 B.C.) Jacob was 85 at Joseph's birth. Jacob was 147 at his death (Gen. 47:28)
    e. **Joseph,** birth 2081 B.C. was sold by his brothers into slavery at seventeen.

        (1).Through these men, we see God's love and power to protect and provide for His people who are obedient to His word.

(2) Note that the time periods are approximate, to give us a general idea of events in relation to time intervals.

3. God planned chosen before Creation, (Gen.1:1-31)

a. BEGINNING.

(1. The name Genesis means "origin," "source" or "beginning." The Hebrew name for the book is **(BERESHITH)** which means, "In the beginning." **(BEGINNING OF ALL THINGS)**

(2. Moses is the author of Genesis. (John 5:46; 7:19.)

(3. Gen. 1:1 "In the beginning God created the heaven and the earth. Now the earth was formless and empty, darkness was over the surface of the deep, and the Spirit of God was hovering over the waters."

(4. vs. 27-God created man in his own image, male and female.

(5. Genesis 3, The fall of man.

(6. Gen. 3:15, God said, "And I will put enmity between you and the woman, and between your offspring and hers; he will crush your head, and you will strike his heel."

(7. **<u>God will give Satan a crushing blow in the resurrection of Jesus.</u>**

(1) Luke 1:39-45; Matt. 1:18-24; Isaiah 53:1-12.

a. Genesis 3:24 God drove man out of the Garden and placed on the east side of the Garden of Eden cherubim and a flaming sword flashing back and forth to guard the way to the tree of life.

4. God's plan of redemption, summed up in Christ (Our Hope) Eph. 1:3-14.

   a. Our hope.

      1. Eph. 3-11.
      2. Col. 1:25028.
      3. Acts 3:18-26.
      4. Acts 26:2-8, 22-23.

   b. **Foreordained, (Summed up all things.-Eph. 1:3-14, note Rom. 8:27-29.)**

      1. Vs. 3-Blessings.
      2. Vs. 5-Adoption.
      3. Vs. 7- Redemption, Grace, Peace, Forgiveness.
      4. Vs. 11- Heritage.
      5. Vs. 13-Salvation.
      6. Vs. 13-Holy Spirit.

   c. **God's plan hidden in the scriptures even the angels desired to know. (I Pet. 1:12.)**

   d. **God's promises:**

      1. Abram (Abraham,) Isaac, Jacob. There were 340 years of the Law of Moses until the seed. (Gal. 3:16.)

         (1).Gal. 3:16 "**The promises were spoken to Abraham and to his seed. The Scripture does not say "and to seeds," meaning many people, but "and to your seed, "meaning one person, who is Christ.**"

      2. A nation, Ex.19:5-6 "**Now if you obey me fully and keep my covenant, then out of all nations you will be my treasured possession. Although the whole earth is mine, you will be for me a kingdom of**

priests and a holy nation. These are the words you are to speak to the Israelites."

3. The prophets point to the cross, I Peter 1:10.-11. **"Concerning this salvation, the prophets, who spoke of the grace that was to come to you, searched intently and with the greatest care, (11) trying to find out the time and circumstances to which the Spirit of Christ in them was pointing when he predicted the sufferings of Christ and the glories that would follow."**

4. Land, (I kings 4:21.)

5. In the New Testament the Spiritual Seed will come. (Jesus Christ and His Church.)

6. Everything was pointing to Christ and His Kingdom, (His Church)

7. The gospel was preached to Abram—(Gal. 3:6-16; 17-29).

CHAPTER 2

THE MYSTERY OF REDEMPTION

OUTLINE OF EPHESIANS

A. Prologue (1:1-2)

B. Praise for God's planned spiritual blessings (1:3-14)
   1. The provision of spiritual blessings (1:3)
   1. The basis of spiritual blessings (1:4-14)

C. Prayer for wisdom and revelation (1:15-23)
   2. Commendation (1:15).
   3. Supplication (1:16-23)

D. **To understand the means of redemption through the death of Christ and His blood you must understand O.T. offering and sacrifice.**

D. **OFFERING AND SACRIFICE FOR SIN In the Old Testament.**

1. **Old Testament-Leviticus 16:5-22.**

   a. The presentation of the animals.

     1). There are two male goats (for a sin offering).

2). One ram (for a burnt offering).

3). A bull (for a sin offering for the High priest and his family.

4). The two goats have to be distinguished-lots will be cast to determine this.

    (a. One for the Lord and one for the scapegoat, (v. 10). The scapegoat shall be presented alive before the Lord to be used for making atonement by sending it into the desert as a scapegoat, and the goat that whose lot falls to the Lord shall be sacrificed as a sin offering.

    (b. **(Christ became that goat that was sacrificed).**

5). The sin offering of the High Priest (Lev. 16:11-14) a bull is killed and its blood is sprinkled on the Mercy Seat for his sins. The sin offering for the people (Lev. 16:15-19) a goat will be killed and its blood sprinkled on the horns of the altar for a burnt offering.

2. The New Testament-Hebrews Chapters 9:11-22; 10:5-10.

    b. The blood of Christ.

        (1. <u>**Ch. 9:11-22, "When Christ came as high priest of the good things that are already here, he went through the greater and more perfect tabernacle that is not man-made, that is to say, not a part of this creation. (12) He did not enter by means of the blood of goats and calves; but he entered the Most Holy Place once for all by his own blood, having obtained eternal redemption. (13) The blood of goats and bulls and the ashes of a heifer sprinkled on those who are ceremonially unclean sanctify them so that they are outwardly clean. (14) How much more, then, will the blood of Christ, who through the eternal Spirit offered himself unblemished to**</u>

God, cleanse our consciences from acts that lead to death, so that we may serve the living God! (15) For this reason Christ is the mediator of a new covenant, that those who are called may receive the promised eternal inheritance-now that the he has died as a ransom to set them free from the sins committed under the first covenant." (16) In the case of a will, it is necessary to prove the death of the one who made it, (17) because a will is in force only when somebody has died; it never takes effect while the *one whom made it is living*. (18) "This is why even the first covenant was not put into effect with out blood. (19) When Moses had proclaimed every commandment of the law to all the people, he took the blood of calves, together with water, scarlet wool and branches of hyssop, and sprinkled the scroll and all the people. (20) He said, "This is the blood of the covenant, which God has commanded you to keep." (21 In the same way, he sprinkled both the tabernacle and everything used in its ceremonies. (22) In fact, the law requires that nearly every thing be cleansed with blood, and without the shedding of blood there is no forgiveness."

(2. Heb; Ch.10:5-10 "Therefore, when Christ came into the world, he said: "Sacrifice and offering you did not desire, but a body you prepared for me; (6) with burnt offerings and sin offerings you were not pleased.

(7) Then I said, 'Here I am-it is written about me in the scroll- I have come to do your will, O God." (8) First he said, "Sacrifices and offerings, burnt offerings and sin offerings you did not desire, nor were you pleased with them" (although the law required them to be made). (9) Then he said, "Here I am, I have come to do your will." He sets aside

**the first to establish the second. (10) And by that
will, we have been made holy through the sacrifice
of the body of Jesus Christ once for all."**

3. **THE MYSTERY OF REDEMPTION IN EPHESIANS!**

A. **Prologue (Eph.1:1-2)**

1. **Vs. 1-2. "Paul, an apostle of Christ Jesus by the
will of God. To the saints in Ephesus, the faithful
in Christ Jesus:" (2) Grace and peace to you from
God our Father and the Lord Jesus Christ."**

a. The saints at Ephesus are a part of the universal
church by virtue of their salvation in Christ.
"Grace" expresses God's steadfast love toward
man and "peace" shows the relational state as
result of that grace. Paul opened his letter to the
church at Ephesus with greetings to the believers
there, expressing his wish that God's grace and
peace be with them. Paul, who wrote this letter,
was an apostle through the will of God. He was
no imposter. His life history, his power to work
miracles and his complete dedication to Christ all
prove that he was a true apostle. See Galatians,
ch. 1 and 2, for Paul's defense of his apostleship.

B. **The mystery of Christ—Eph. 3:1-6**

1. **Eph. 3:1-6 "For this reason I, Paul, the prisoner of
Christ Jesus for the sake of you Gentiles. Surely
you have heard about the administration of God's
grace that was given to me for you. In reading this,
then, you will be able to understand my insight in
to the mystery of Christ. (5) Which was not made
known to men in other generations as it has now
been revealed by the Spirit to God's holy apostles
and prophets.**

(6) This mystery is that through the gospel the Gentiles are heirs together with Israel, members together of one body, and sharers together in the promise in Christ Jesus." (See Acts 23:18)

a. **God** called His plan a mystery. The whole scheme of God's redemption was kept locked up in the mind of God. The knowledge of God's mind cannot be known except through revelation. His plan was kept hidden, until through revelation, was given to Paul and now through Paul's writings. Now we can know God's plan that was hidden (Revelation's meaning, "to take the cape off".) The book is the mind of God. The words **for this reason** (also used in v. 14) specifically point back to 2:11-22, which dealt with the Jewish and Gentile believers, being raised to new heights. But they also more generally refer back to all the first part of the epistle in which Paul discussed God's grace to the Gentiles. The words **"I, Paul, the prisoner of Christ Jesus for the sake of you Gentiles",** is pointing to Paul's imprisonment in Rome because of his service for Christ (cf. 4:1; 2 Tim. 1:8; Phil. 1, 9), and more particularly because of his ministry as the **apostle to the Gentiles** (2 Tim. 1:11-12). Because of Paul's faithfulness to God, God has given him to be the stewardship among the Gentiles (Eph. 3:2) **(2)**

b. From creation the mystery hidden till Christ on the cross. **(Eph. 3:2-5; Col. 1:25; Rom. 16:25-26; I Cor. 2:1-7.**

c. **Rom. 16:25-26 "Now to him who is able to establish you by my gospel and the proclamation of Jesus Christ, according to the revelation of the mystery hidden for long ages past, but now revealed and made known through the**

prophetic writings by the command of the
eternal God, so that all nations might believe
and obey him"

**(1. The Prophets sought and the Angels desire,
(I Pet.1:9-13; I Cor. 2:7-9.
(2. Received by the Spirit (I Cor. 2:10-13; Eph.
3:3-11; Col. 1:24-28.**

d. Paul will explain the mystery of Christ (Eph.
3:5-6) and then they would understand. His
"insight" was not his own discovery; it was
revealed to him by God.

e. Paul further explains that **the mystery** is the
"grace" mentioned in verse 2. The mystery that was
unknown is not defined till verse 6. The mystery's
disclosure was given to Paul **by revelation,** which
in fact he had **already written briefly** about, not
in another epistle, but in this one (in 2:11-22).
Some take this meaning that the mystery was
partially revealed in the Old Testament but is now
fully revealed after the Church was established.
This mystery was revealed **by the Spirit** (cf. Eph.
2:22), and its recipients were **God's apostles and
prophets** (cf. 2:20; 4:11). Some have promoted
the idea that this revelation was given to Paul,
but Eph. 3:5 explicitly states that it was given
to the apostles and prophets and that Paul was
one who was to sow the seed of God's plan of
redemption.

C. The constitution of the mystery Eph. 3:6.

a. Paul now defined the **mystery,** he stated that the
Gentile believers with the Jewish believers **are** (a)
heirs together "fellow heirs," 2:19, kjv) of God's
riches (1:3-14), (b) are the same **body** (cf. 2:16;

<u>syssōma</u> occurs only in 3:6 in the NT), **and** (c) are **sharers together in the promise** (the messianic promise; cf. 2:12; Gal. 3:29) The mystery is not something mysterious, but is a secret hidden in the O.T. past but now has been revealed. This is made possible **through the gospel.** Believing Jews and **Gentiles** are in **one** body and joined together through believing in Jesus Christ.

b. Note Colossians 1:24-29. ". . . **The mystery that has been kept hidden for ages and generations, but is now disclosed to the saints."**
   (1).**Col. 1:27 "To them God has chosen to make known among the Gentiles the glorious riches of this mystery, which is Christ in you, the hope of glory."**

D. **The provision of spiritual blessings.**

  1. **Praise for God's planned spiritual blessings—Eph.1:3-14.**

    a. <u>**Vs 3 "Praise be to God and Father of our Lord Jesus Christ, who has blessed us in the heavenly realms with every spiritual blessing in Christ"**</u>

    b. Paul now moved from his general greeting to the saints at Ephesus to an expanded discussion of the reason God is to be praised—because of the spiritual blessings He has planned for believers in Christ. **Peace is the result of grace.** The praise should be given **to the God and Father of our Lord Jesus Christ.** In Ephesians 1:2 God is the Father of believers; here in verse 3 God is the Father of Christ (cf. v. 17). In Ephesians 1:2 the first Person of the Trinity belongs to believers, suggested by the word "our." Here in verse 3 the pronoun "our" shows that believers belong to Christ, the second Person of the Godhead. Since He is the Son of God and believers are connected with Him, they are also related to the Father. Paul's use of the past tense participle "has blessed" points to this blessing or prospering of believers as having occurred in the past.

c. (Not only the N.T. believers blessed but those in the O.T. that by faith believe are blessed.) With what are believers blessed? **With every spiritual blessing** (in the Gr., this phrase precedes the words "in the heavenly realms"). "Every spiritual blessing" *(eulo*

d. The Father's initiative Redemption is viewed three ways:

(1) Father's plan, Eph. 1:3-14.
(2) Father's price, His Son. Eph.1:1-12.
(3) Father's pledge, the seal of the Holy Spirit. Eph.1:13-14

E. God's plan for redemption in Christ (Eph.1:4-14).

1. Eph. 1:4-8 <u>"For he chose us in him before the creation of the world to be holy and blameless in his sight. In love (5) he predestined us to be adopted as his sons through Jesus Christ, in accordance with his pleasure and will- (6) to the praise of his glorious grace, which he has freely given us in the One he loves. (7) In him we have redemption through his blood, the forgiveness of sins, in accordance with the riches of God's grace (8) that he lavished on us with all wisdom and understanding."</u>

a. The apostle first told when God's work of election took place: before the Creation of the world. (Note I Peter 1:20) The idea is that spiritual blessings (1:3) for believers are *because of,* or on the basis of the work of the God -Head: God blesses believers because of the (1) Fathers plan 1-14 (Son's dying, Rom. 5:1-5), and the (2) (Spirit's sealing 1;.13-14). Both concepts seem to be included: spiritual blessings are the work of the three Persons of the Godhead. Long ago, even before God created the world, God decided, "The people who accept and obey Him, shall be My chosen people." God did not choose certain individuals to go to heaven and others to go to hell. How did God choose His people? **(Galatians 3:26-29** "You are all sons of God through faith in Christ Jesus, for all of you who were baptized into Christ have clothed yourselves with Christ. There is neither Jew nor Greek, slave nor free, male nor female, for you are all in him, Christ Jesus, if you belong to Christ then you are Abraham's seed, and heirs according to the promise." **He chose those who are in Christ to be His people. (3)**

b. Vs. 5-The cause of election is God's predestination of believers unto Sonship (cf. "predestined" in v. 11). Predestined is from *proorisas,* "marked out beforehand. The emphasis of predestination is more on *(the what rather the "who")* in that the believers' predetermined destiny is their being adopted as full-fledged sons of God through Jesus Christ. The idea of adoption is also found in Romans 8:15, 23; Galatians 4:4-7. In adoption a son is brought into a family and is given the same rights as a child who is born into that family. Rom 8:30 "And those whom he predestined he also called, and those whom he called he also justified, and those whom he justified he also glorified." Verb, aorist, passive, nominative predestined Eph 1:11 "In him we have obtained an inheritance, having been predestined according to the purpose of him who works all things according to the counsel of his will,"

d. Vs. 7. Redemption (apolytrōsin) bought back for a price (Heb. 9:22) or returned to the rightful owner or delivered from slavery to freedom. In this case from sin (cf. Col. 1:14; Rom. 3:24, 8:15; Heb. 9:15, 11:35. The same idea is seen in some of the other verses where this Greek word appears (Rom. 3:24; 8:23; 1 Cor. 1:30,) because sin separates man from God. The means of redemption (bought back) is the death of Christ (through His blood; cf. Eph. 2:13; 1 Peter 1:19), which completely satisfied God's justice (Rom. 3:24-25). This was accomplished in accordance with the riches of God's grace (cf. Eph. 1:6; 2:7). The cost of Christ's blood is the measure of the wealth of God's unmerited favor to every believer. It was accomplished "according to" (*kata*) the wealth of His grace (cf. Phil. 4:19). Six times in Ephesians Paul referred to God's riches (1:7, 18; 2:4, 7; 3:8, 16). God's grace is given to enable believers to understand His will. God gives them wisdom (*sophia;* cf. v. 17; 3:10; Col. 1:9, 28; 2:3, 23; 3:16; 4:5), objective insight into the true nature of God's revelation. **(4)**

4. **Eph. 1; 9-10 "And he made known to us the mystery of his will according to his good pleasure, which he purposed in Christ, (10) to be put into effect when the times will have reached their fulfillment- to bring all things in heaven and on earth together under one head, even Christ**.

   a. <u>Vs. 9</u>-Down through all the ages men have invented all kinds of religions and philosophies in an effort to discover what is really the truth! So believers are able to grasp something of the purpose of it all. The final truth was revealed through Jesus Christ, This is accomplished because God made known to us the mystery of His will (cf. "will" in Eph.1:1, 5, 11). "Mystery" is a truth unveiled by God's revelation (cf. Rom. 16:25.)

b. Vs. 10- God's will is to be put into effect when the times will have reached their fulfillment. Literally, when God's plan would be summed up in Christ.

5. **Eph. 1:11-12 "In him we were also chosen, having been predestined according to the plan of him who works out every thing in conformity with the purpose of his will, (12) in order that we, who were the first to hope in Christ, might be for the praise of his glory."**

   a. **Vs.11-**In whom (Christ) we Jews, as well as you Gentiles, were made a heritage, a private possession for God, having been foreordained to this honor not by being an Abrahamic descent and the law, but according to that pre-planned program which God, who does all things, according to the counsel of His will, laid out in Christ, as a result of the insight of God's blessing and into the mystery of His will (vv.8-10). In foreordaining us to be His heritage, God was working toward the purpose that we would be a people devoted to praising His glory. The Jews were the first to have hoped in the Messiah (or Christ). (cf. Acts 3:26; Rom. 1:16.) Both Jews and Gentiles had access to God's blessing; the Jews were called first (cf. Acts 3:26; Rom. 1:16).

   b. Vs.12-The words "for the praise of His glory" serve as a regularly recurring phrase used after a description of the work of each Person of the Godhead (cf. vv. 6, 14).

6. **Eph.1:13-14 "And you also were included in Christ when you heard the word of truth, the gospel of your salvation. Having believed, you were marked in him with a seal, the promised Holy Spirit, (14) who is a deposit guaranteeing our inheritance until the redemption of those who are God's possession- to the praise of his glory."**

a. **"You heard the word of truth"**-John 8:32 "Then you will know the truth, and the truth will set you free."

b. **Vs. 13-14** Also refers to the Gentiles in contrast with the Jews (cf. comments on vv. 11-12). When they heard the Word of truth (cf. Col. 1:5; 2 Tim. 2:15; James 1:18) which is further described as "the gospel of your salvation," and believed, they were sealed with the promised Holy Spirit.

The KJV says that the sealing occurs "after" the hearing and believing, thus connoting a second work of grace. This is wrong, for believers are sealed at the moment they hear and believe and obey the Word of truth (Gospel.0 When we (1) heard the Word of truth, the gospel, and (2) believed it (and, of course, we were baptized; Gal. 3:26-27), God gave us the gift of the Holy Spirit (Acts 2:38). Then the Holy Spirit in the Christian stamps and seals him as being "God's property." **(4) Logos Bible Software, Libronix Digital Library System (The Bible Knowledge Commentary) (5)**

7. **A broader look at God's work of redemption:**

(1. Eternity-God planned it (Eph. 1:11,)We are chosen by God, according to the foreknowledge of God the Father. (I Peter 1:1-2,)

(2. Time-1.called, 2. Justified, 3. Works sanctification Rom. 8:29-30; 2 Thess. 2:10; Phil. 2:12-13.

(3. Future- Eternity-1. Glorification Eph. 1:2, 6:12,14.

CHAPTER 3

HISTORY OF ABRAHAM

The patriarchal period. (From the birth of Abraham to the
Death of Joseph; Gen. 11:27-Ch. 50.

I. THE HISTORY OF ABRAHAM IS RECORDED IN GENESIS- CHAPTERS 12-Ch.15.

A. The patriarch Abraham, who was the head of the chosen
   family, was born about 2166 B.C. and died 1991 B.C.
B. The promise made to Abraham. Gen. 12:1-9.
C. The same promise to Isaac Gen. 26:1-6.
D. The same promise to Jacob Gen. 28:10-15.

    1. With the problem of sin persisting, God acted to
   call Abraham to make a covenant with him and
   his descendants (2,100 B.C. Gen. 12:1-1; 24). The
   covenant was renewed and confirmed through a
   series of events which led to the establishment of
   circumcision as a sign (15:1-17:27). Other events
   from Abraham's life are related, and the marriage
   of Isaac to Rebekah occurs (Gen. 22:20-24:67). A
   final account of the posterity of Abraham is given
   (25:19-26) Isaac, (Gen. 27-36). Isaac was the father
   of Esau and Jacob (Gen. 25:19-28). The older son sold
   his birthright to the younger (Gen. 25:29-34). Some

events of controversy in Isaac's life are related (Gen. 26:17-33), and the marriages of Esau are recorded (Gen. 34-35). Jacob, Gen. 27-36, After a series of unfortunate events in his father's home (27:1-46), Jacob left home as an exile and had an encounter with the Lord in which the Abrahamic covenant and promise was renewed in him (28:1-22). The posterity of both, Jacob and Esau is recorded (35:21-36:43).The nation of Israel emerged from Jacob's descendants. Gen. 37-50—Jacob's son Joseph, (Gen. 37-50) Joseph's dream (37:1-26) and Judah's experience with Tamar are told (38:1-30). Attention then focuses on Joseph's life in Egypt. Providential events exalted him under Pharaoh (39:1-41:57). Here he encountered his brothers again (42:1-45:15). Joseph called his father to Egypt and was reunited with his family (45:16-47:26). The last days of Jacob are related (47:27-50:14), along with Joseph's assurances of forgiveness to his brothers (50:15-26). Genesis closes with the Israelites prospering in Egypt.

E. **Genesis, the book of origins, set the stage for the great story of redemption.**

    1. <u>**Gen. 12:1-3 "The Lord said to Abram, "Leave your country, your people and your father's household and go to the land I will show you. (2) I will make you into a great nation and I will bless you; I will make your name great, and you will be a blessing. (3) I will bless those who bless you, and whoever curses you I will curse; and all people on earth will be blessed through you."**</u>

        a. The promise had three elements, and were based on God's call for Abram to leave his land: **(a)** a great nation, (Ex.19) **(b)** a blessing for Abram, and **(c)** a great name (v. 2). These promises would enable him to "be a blessing," based on this obedience were God's three promises: **Vs.1-3** Record God's call to **Abram,** and verses 4-9 record Abram's obedience.

1) A great nation would arise from his descendants.

2) The land of Canaan would be possessed by his descendants.

3) Vs 3, "all the people of the earth will be blessed," involve the crowning blessing of the Old Covenant, the Promise of the Messiah to, "All families of the earth" that includes Jews and Gentiles. (Acts 3:25; Gal. 3:8). All nations would be blessed through his seed. God would make his name great and he would be a blessing to the world. Abram's calling had a purpose: his obedience would bring great blessing to: (a) **bless those who** blessed him, (b) **curse** anyone who would treat him lightly, and (c) bless the families of the **earth** through him (v. 3). To bless or curse Abram was to bless or curse Abram's God. The greatest fulfillment is the fact that Jesus Christ became the means of blessing to the world (Gal. 3:8, 16; cf. Rom. 9:5). The idea of faith is stressed in these passages. Abram was told to leave several things—his **"country, his people,** and his **father's household."** (Gen. 12:1). But he was told nothing about the land to which he must go. His departure required an act of faith. **"I will make of you a great nation, and I will bless you, and make your nane great, and you shall be a blessing to others; and I will bless them that bless you, and curse him that curse you, and in you shall all families of the earth be blessed," (Gen. 12:2-3)**

The last words already involve the crowning blessing of the Old Covenant, the promise of the

Messiah, and that to the Gentiles, "all families of the earth" Acts 3:25; Gal. 3:8)

F. All features of the promise have been completely fulfilled;

> a. The nation promise-Israel, Gen. 32:27-28:cf. Ex. 19-20.
>
> b. The land promise-Possessed under Joshua, Josh, 21:43-45.
>
> c. The seed promise- Jesus Christ, Gal. 3:16.

1. **Gen. 12:4-9 "So Abram left, as the Lord had told him; and Lot went with him. Abram was seventy-five years old when he set out from Haran. (5) He took his wife Sarai, his nephew Lot, all the possessions they had accumulated and the people they had acquired in Haran, and they set out for the land of Canaan, and They arrived there. (6) Abram traveled through the land as far as the site of the great tree of Moreh at Shechem. At that time the Canaanites were in the land. (7) The Lord appeared to Abram and said, "To your offspring I will give this land." So he built an altar there to the Lord, who had appeared to him. (8) From there he went on toward the hills east of Bethel and pitched his tent, with Bethel on the west and Ai on the east. There he built an altar to the Lord and called on the name of the Lord. (9) Then Abram set out and continued toward the Negev."**

> a. **Vs.4-6** Abram now left Mesopotamia and crossed the Great River, the Euphrates (called the flood in Josh. 24:2). This separated him entirely from his old home, and possibly accounts for the title Hebrew which he came to wear (Gen. 14:13). While some think that the name Hebrew came from the patriarch

Eber (Gen. 11:16, it may come from the Hebrew verb meaning to 'cross over.' He was a blessing (vv. 5-9). In Haran many people ("souls" K.J.V.) were acquired by Abram and his family (v. 5).

b. Vs.7-9Then in the land of Canaan he built altars at Shechem (v. 6) and east of Bethel (v. 8). At this second location he called on the name of the Lord, that is, he called on Yahweh by name (cf. 21:33; 26:25).

Luther translated this verb "preached"; he was not far off. So God had a witness in the midst of the Canaanites. For Israel the call of their great patriarch demonstrated that their promises were from God, promises of a great nation, a land, divine blessing, and sovereign protection. Yahweh's appearance and confirmation (v. 7) proved that Canaan was their destiny. But God demanded a response by faith if this generation were to share in those promised blessings. Faith takes God at His word and obeys Him. **(Heb. 11:6-"And without faith it is impossible to please God, because anyone who comes to him must believe that he exists and that he rewards those who earnestly seek him.") (6)**

CHAPTER 4

THE HISTORY of JACOB and JOSEPH

THE HISTORY OF THE PATRIARCH -Their sojourn in Egypt Genesis 12:10-20 and Israel became a nation of people.

1. **<u>Gen, 12:10</u>.**-This sojourn has much more to it than a simple lesson in honesty—though the story certainly warns against the folly of deceit. The claim that she is "my sister" occurs three times in the patriarchal narratives (v. 13; 20:2; 26:7). Critics say these occasions refer to the same event. However, in the second instance Abram explained that this was their policy wherever they went (20:13) so it is not surprising that he repeated this lie. One cannot miss the deliberate parallelism between this sojourn of Abram in Egypt and the later event in the life of the nation in bondage in Egypt. The motifs are remarkably similar: the famine in the land (12:10; 47:13), the descent to Egypt to sojourn (12:10; 47:27), the attempt to kill the males but save the females (12:12; Ex. 1:22). The plagues on Egypt (Gen. 12:17; Ex. 7:14-11:10), the spoiling of Egypt (Gen. 12:16; Ex. 12:35-36), the deliverance (Gen. 12:19; Ex. 15), and the ascent to the Negev (Gen. 13:1; Num. 13:17, 22). The great deliverance out of bondage that Israel experienced was already accomplished in her ancestor, and probably was a source of comfort and encouragement to them. God was doing more than just promise deliverance for the future nation; it was as if in anticipation He acted

out their deliverance in Abram. In relation to the message of the book, Genesis 12:10-20 is significantly placed right after Abram's call and obedience. In this story Abram was not walking by faith as he had been in the beginning, but God had made promises to him and would keep them. Abram was not the only patriarch who had to be rescued from such difficulties.

A. JACOB AND JOSEPH IN EGYPT Gen. 27-50.

a. Jacob gets Isaac's blessing, chapter 27-28.
b. Jacob's name change to Israel, Genesis 32:28 and is united with his brother Esau.33:1-28.
c. Joseph's boyhood (37:1-26) and Judah's experience with Tamar are told.
d. Joseph's life in Egypt and the events that exalted him under Pharaoh (39:1-41:57).
e. Genesis closes with the Israelites prospering in Egypt.

1. Judah: Let Him (God) be praised.

a. Son of Jacob and Leah—Gen. 29:15-35.
b. Ancestor to Christ—Matt. 1:3-6.
c. Jacob gives birthright to Judah—Gen. 49:8-12.

2. Gen. 49:8-12 "Judah, your brothers will praise you; your hand will be on the neck of your enemies; your father's sons will bow down to you. (9) You are a lion's cub, O Judah; you return from the prey, my son. Like a lion he crouches and lies down, like a lioness-who dares to rouse him? (10) "The scepter will not depart from Judah, nor the ruler's staff from between his feet, until he comes to whom it belongs and the obedience of the nations is his." (11) He will tether his donkey to a vine, his colt to the choicest branch; he will wash his garments in wine, his robes in the blood of grapes, (12) His eyes will be darker than wine, his teeth whiter than milk.

a. The oracle pivots on the word **until** (49:10b). When the Promised One who will rule the nations appears, the scene will become an earthly paradise. These verses anticipate the kingship in Judah culminating in the reign of Messiah (cf. the tribe of Judah, Rev. 5:5), in which **nations** will obey Him. **The scepter will not depart from Judah . . . until He comes.** Judah is to be the leader, "the lion." As the lions is king of the forest, so was Judah to have royal sovereignty, through David onwards to the Son of David, the SHILOH, into whom, as "the Lion of the tribe of Judah, "all nations should render homage and obedience. The whole description here is full of Messianic overtones. They applied to David (Psalms 89:20-37), and from him carried forward in prophecy, through Psalms. 72. (Isa 9;11, to Ezek. 21:27), till they were finally realized in Jesus Christ, "sprung out of Judah, (Heb. 7:14),

"For he himself is our peace, who has made the two one", (Eph. 2:14-16), For he, "has put everything under his feet, (I Cor. 15:25), ". . . See the Lion of the tribe of Judah, the Root of David, has triumphed." (Rev. 5:5). **(7)**

B. **Jacob gets Isaac's blessing, God's promise. And Jacob is united with Esau Gen. 27-32.**

1. **Chapters, 27-29- Isaac's blessing, and God's promise of Abraham is given to Jacob.**

2. Ezekiel 21:26 "this is what the Sovereign Lord says; "Take off the turban, remove the crown. It will not be as it was. The lowly will be exalted and the exalted will be brought low. A ruin! I will make it a ruin! It will not be restored". It was addressed to the last king of Judah.

3. Genesis chapter 25:24-34. "Will set the stage of God's plan for His promises to Abraham.

4. Gen. 25:19-23; The account of Abraham's son Isaac.

5. V. 21; "Isaac prayed for his wife Rebekah, because she was barren.

Gen.25:24-34 ; "**When the time came for her to give birth, there were twin boys in her womb. (25) The first to come out was red, and his whole body was like a hairy garment; so they named him Esau. (26 After this, his brother came out, with his hand grasping Esau's heel; so he was named Jacob. Isaac was sixty years old when Rebekah gave birth to them. (27) The boys grew up, and Esau became a skillful hunter, a man of the open country, while Jacob was a quiet man, staying among the tents. (28) Isaac, who had a taste for wild game, loved Esau, but Rebekah loved Jacob. (29) Once when Jacob was cooking some stew, Esau came in from the open country, famished. (30) He said to Jacob, "Quick, let me have some of that red stew! I'm famished!" (That is why he was called Edom,) (31) Jacob replied, "First sell me your birthright." (32) "Look, I am about to die," Esau said. "What good is the birthright to me?" (33) But Jacob said, "Swear to me first." So he swore an oath to him, selling his birthright to Jacob.(34) Then Jacob gave Esau some bread and some lentil stew. He ate and drank, and then got up and left. So Esau despised his birthright."**

a. The oldest man in a family was to get the largest part of the family estate when the Father dies.

b. It was not until years later that Rebekah, whose barrenness was removed through the prayers of Isaac, bore twin sons, Esau (hairy) or Edom (the Red), and Jacob (the Supplanter) whose future destiny was prophetically signified by the strange incident which accompanied their birth. Their struggle in the womb portended the deadly animosity of the two nations that were to spring from them. And the grasp of the younger on the elder's heel foreshadowed the way that Jacob would take hold of his brother's birthright and blessing, and supplant him as the main family heir. Their physical appearance was as different as their characters afterward proved; the ruddy and hairy Esau became a rough, wild hunter; the smooth Jacob a quiet denizen of the tent. These differences of character were fostered by the foolish partiality of their parents, the great curse of all family life; "Isaac loved Esau, because he did eat his venison; but Rebekah loved Jacob" (Gen. 15:21-28). It is important to observe that God chose Jacob, the younger, to be over his brother Esau before they were born. Before the children were born, neither having done anything good or bad, it was God's declared purpose that the older should serve the younger (Rom. 9:10-13; Gen. 25:25-23) . . . And assuredly the characters of Jacob and of Esau that subsequently emerged showed God's wisdom and foreknowledge in choosing Jacob.

c. **Genesis Chapter 27:1-27 Vs.** vs.1-4 (*Isaac and Esau*)—**Isaac** offered to bless **Esau.** Important notes are given here about Isaac's **weak** eyesight and **old** age, and his love for **wild game** and **tasty food** (ch.27:1-29), governed his heart. But because Isaac was going to give Esau his blessing, this was a problem for Rebekah that prompted her to take action if she was to help Jacob.

d. **Vs. 5-17** (*Rebekah and Jacob*)—**Rebekah** sent **Jacob** into action to stop **Isaac.** Rebekah seemed certain she could duplicate the taste of meat from wild **game** with goat's meat (v. 9). But **Jacob** was not so sure he could deceive his father. After all, Jacob said, if Isaac touched him, Isaac would know the difference between Esau's **hairy** skin and Jacob's **smooth skin.** Jacob had no guilt—only fear—regarding the plan.

But the **blessing** was in danger and all must be risked, including even the possibility of **a curse** on **Rebekah** (vv.

12-13). So **Jacob** did as **his mother** told him. **Rebekah** even had **Jacob** put on some of Esau's **best clothes!**

e. Vs. __18-29__ *(Jacob and Isaac)*—Jacob deceived **his father** and obtained the blessing. Prodded by his mother **Jacob** lied twice to his father, first, about his identity (**I am Esau**, v. 19), and second, that **God** had given him **success** (in hunting, v. 20). Three times the old man voiced his suspicion (vv. 20, 22, 24). But deceived by his senses of touch (vv. 16, 23) and smell (v. 27), **he blessed** Jacob, thinking he was **Esau** (vv. 27:27-29). The blessing included prosperity in crops (v. 28), domination over other nations and his brothers (cf. v. 37), cursing on those who **cursed** him, and blessing on those who **blessed** him (v. 29).

f. **Vs. 30-37** *(Esau and Isaac)*- When Esau brought in his **food,** emotions ran high. **Isaac trembled violently** over what had happened and **Esau** was very **bitter** and angry (v. 34). So in a sense Rebekah and Jacob won, though they gained nothing that God would not have given them anyway; and they lost much. Yet God would work through their deceitfulness. Their activities only succeeded in doing what God's oracle had predicted. God's program will triumph, often in spite of human activities. The story is one of parental favoritism, which tore their family completely apart. The story is also an account of spiritual insensitivity. Jacob will flee from Esau vs.42 "When Rebekah was told what her older son Esau had said, (vs. 42, "I will kill my brother Jacob.") she sent for her younger son Jacob and said to him, "Your brother Esau is consoling himself with the thought of killing you. Now then, my son do, what I say; Flee at once . . ."

C. Jacob's name change to Israel and is united with Esau, Genesis 32-33.

    a. Ch. 32:1-2, God prepared Jacob for meeting Esau by giving the patriarch a vision of angels. Jacob had just left Laban and was about to return to the land and face Esau once again. At this point God's invisible world openly touched Jacob's visible world. The encounter is described with striking brevity. Four Hebrew words report the meeting: **the angels of God met him. Jacob** then **named** the **place Mahanaim,** possibly meaning "two camps."

He must have seen the camp of angels as a source of comfort to his own camp as he prepared to reenter the land.

    b. **Vs. 3-8,** Prompted by the idea in the vision, **Jacob sent messengers** to **Esau** in **Edom.** (The Heb. word for "angels" also means "messengers.") Many key ideas and wordplays are in this section. **Jacob** had just seen the angels (God's messengers) and now he sent his own messengers to **Esau.** He had recognized the angels as "the camp **(maḥănēh)** of God," he had named the place maḥănāyim (v. 2), and then (out of **fear** of **Esau** who was **coming** toward him with **400 men**) he **divided** his family **into two groups** or camps. After wrestling with God, Jacob's name was changed to Israel-Gen. 32:

    c. **Gen. 32:26-28, "The man said, "Let me go, for it is daybreak, but Jacob replied, "I will not let you go unless you bless me." (27) The man asked him, "What is your name?" "Jacob" he answered. (28) Then the man said, "Your name will no longer be Jacob, but Israel, because you have struggled with God and with man and have overcome."**

D. JACOB MEETS ESAU -GENESIS CH.33, AND THEY ARE UNITED.

a. **Gen. 33 vs.1-7.** Jacob was fearful when he was about to met **Esau.** He lined up his **children** and wives, with **Rachel and Joseph in the rear.** The contrasts between the two brothers, as they met after 20 years, are interesting. (v. 3), Jacob halted and bowed to the ground seven times showing homage toward Esau while on his way to meet him. **Esau,** however, eagerly **ran to meet Jacob and embraced him . . . kissed him,** and **they** both **wept.** In talking with Esau, Jacob constantly referred to himself as **your servant** or "his servant" (vv. 5, 14) and to his brother as "my lord" (vv. 8, 13-15) whereas **Esau** simply called **Jacob** "my brother" (v. 9).

b. <u>Gen. 33:8-11,</u> **Jacob** pressed **Esau** to accept the gift of 550 animals (cf. 32:13-15). When Esau hesitated to accept the livestock, Jacob insisted. He said, **accept this,** "my" **gift (minḥātî,)** the same word he used in 32:13. Then Jacob added, **accept** "my" present **(birkātî).** The word "present" comes from **(bārak),** "to bless." By using **(birkātî), Jacob** showed that he was deliberately wanting to share his blessing with **Esau,** trying to soften his earlier actions. Having lived through that, he then survived Esau. **Esau** was changed from seeking revenge to desiring reconciliation._These changes were proof that God had answered Jacob's prayer (32:11). **(8)**

E. THE SETTLEMET AT SHECHEM-GEN. 33:18-20.

a. <u>Gen. 33:18-20</u> These verses form sort of a concluding section of Jacob's sojourn outside the land. He returned in peace and camped near **Shechem,** directly west of the Jabbok River and about 20 miles from the Jordan **in Canaan.** This is where Abram first camped when he arrived in Canaan (Gen. 12:6). Jacob once more crossed the Jordan, "and came in peace" to the city of Shechem, which is in the land of Canaan. But the country had changed since Abram entered the land, and made this his first resting-place. There was no city there, and it was only "the place of **Shechem.**" From "the children of Hamor" Jacob bought the field where he "spread his tent." This was "the portion" which Jacob afterwards gave to his son Joseph, and here the "bones of Joseph, which the children of Israel brought out of Egypt.

b. **SHECHEM-**(Heb. sheckhem, shoulder), a personal name and the name of a district and city in the hill-country of Ephraim in north central Palestine.

F. THE SELLING OF JOSEPH INTO EGYPT GEN. 37:2-36).

1. The dreams of Joseph (37:2-11).

a. Jacob lived in the land where his father had stayed, the land of Canaan. (2) This is the account of Jacob. Joseph, a young man of seventeen, was tending the flocks with his brothers, the sons of Bilhah and the sons of Zilpah, his father's wives, and he brought their father a bad report about them.

(3) Now Israel loved Joseph more than any of his other sons, because he had been born to him in his old age; and he made a richly ornamented robe for him. We must remember that the birth of Benjamin and Rachel's death occurred only five or six years before Joseph was sold into Egypt. For the proper understanding of what follows it is necessary to remember that what may be called the PERSONAL history of the patriarch ceases with Jacob; or rather that it now merges into that of the CHILDREN of Israel; of the family, and of the tribes.

1. **Gen. 37:2-4 "This is the account of Jacob. Joseph, a young man of seventeen, was tending the flock with his brothers, the sons of Bilhah and the sons of Zilpah, his father's wives, and he brought their father a bad report about them. (3) Now Israel loved Joseph more than any of his other sons, because he had been born to him in his old age; and he made a richly ornamented robe for him." (4) When his brothers saw that their father loved him more than any of them, they hated him and could not speak a kind word to him."**

    a. When Jacob made for Joseph a special dress, this seems to signify that Jacob favored him above the rest with the intent of granting him all or a larger portion of the inheritance. For Joseph was the firstborn of Rachel, Jacob's loved wife (30:22-24). "His brethren hated him, and could not speak peaceably unto him." (K.J.V.) To increase their hatred, Joseph dreamed two dreams (Gen. 36:11). **(9)**

2. **Gen.37:5-11 "Joseph had a dream, and when he told it to his brothers, they hated him all the more. (6) He said to them, "Listen to this dream I had; (7) we were binding sheaves of grain out in the field when suddenly my sheaf rose and stood upright, while your sheaves gathered around mine and bowed down to it." (8) His brothers said to him, "Do you intend to reign over us? Will you actually rule us?" And they hated him all the more because of his dream and what he had said. (9) Then he had another dream, and he told it to his brothers, "Listen, "he said, "I had another dream, and this time the sun and moon and eleven stars were bowing down to me."**

    (10) When he told his father as well as his brothers, his father rebuked him and said, "What is this dream you had? "Will your mother and I and your brothers actually come and bow down to the ground before you? (11) His

brothers were jealous of him, but his father kept the matter in mind."

a. In Old Testament times the people invested in dreams and believed in them. God confirmed Jacob's choice of his faithful son by two dreams. God's revelation was given in different forms in the Old Testament. He used dreams when His people were leaving or outside the land, that is, in the land of pagans. When Jacob made for Joseph a special dress, "his brothers hated him, and could not speak peaceably to him". To increase their hatred, Joseph dreamed two dreams. And by the two dreams God predicted that Joseph would rule over his family. **(1). In Joseph's first** dream his brothers' sheaves of corn bow down to his, which stood upright in their midst; a most fitting, not only their submission to him, but of their submission to him for grain in Egypt. **(2) The second dream** was of wider and higher import. It included his father and his mother, as will as his brethren (now specified as eleven), in the reverence done to him and the emblems chosen leave little doubt that the dream prefigured the homage of all nature, Him whose sign was the star of Bethlehem, (Jesus) and of whom Joseph was one of the clearest types. Joseph's brothers were determined to prevent any such humiliation, even if this meant killing Joseph (Gen. 37:18).

(1. In a dream God had announced to Abraham the Egyptian bondage in the first place (15:13); in a dream God promised protection and prosperity for Jacob in his sojourn with Laban (28:12, 15).

(2. Jacob pondered the matter (v. 11). He was well aware that God's will would be done even if it would be through his younger son to rule over the elder, and that God could declare His choice in advance by even a dream. **(10)**

G. The sale of Joseph-Gen. 37:12-36.

a. **Gen.37:12 and 18. "Now his brothers had gone to graze their father's flocks near Shechem, and Israel said to Joseph, "As you know, your brothers are grazing the flocks near Shechem. Come, I am going to send you to them." "Very well," he replied . . . . (17b-18) ". . . So Joseph went after his brothers and found them near Dothan. But they saw him in the distance, and before he reached them, they plotted to kill him."**

b. In spite of the hatred Joseph knew they held for him, he complied with his father's wishes. From Jacob's home in the Valley of Hebron (v. 14) north to Shechem (v. 12) was about 50 miles, and Dothan was another 15 miles north.

c. Gen. 37:18-24 The brothers plot to kill Joseph the dreamer in order to prevent his dreams from being fulfilled. Note his brothers' attitude. Before, they plotted to kill many Shechemites in revenge for their sister (34:24-29); now, they plotted to kill their own brother! His life was saved by Reuben; who persuaded them to avoid the actual shedding of Joseph's blood by casting him into an empty pit. Ruben intended to take him and restore him to his father. So the brothers stripped Joseph of his robe and threw him into a dry cistern to die. And then sat down to eat their meal.

d. Gen.37:25-28. Just then an Ishmaelite caravan was seen on the road which leads from Mount Gilead through Dothan to Egypt, carrying spices and gums of the Syrian Desert. After Reuben having left them, v.22, Judah begin prompting his brothers to sell Joseph to the Ishmaelites who took him to Egypt (v.28). The term Ishmaelites became a general designation for desert tribes, so those Midianite traders were also known as Ishmaelites. Joseph was treated bitterly by his brothers; but being sold for 20 shekels (8 ounces of silver) and taken to Egypt was in God's plan.

e. Gen.37:29-36 Reuben vs.29 tried to save Joseph but was too late, he will be rewarded later. The theme of deception again surfaced in the family; here Jacob was deceived once again—this time by his own sons They carried back Joseph's robe dipped it in a kid's (young goat) blood, to deceive Jacob into thinking that Joseph was dead, that a wild beast had killed and eaten him. Jacob mourned greatly over the loss of his beloved son (tearing one's clothes and wearing sackcloth [animal skins] were signs of grief and mourning; (vs.34)

f. Gen. 37:36 "Meanwhile, the Midianites sold Joseph in Egypt to Potiphar, one of Pharaoh's officials, the captain of the guard." From this time on the history of God's plan of redemption through His chosen family entertains itself with the mighty kingdom of Egypt. It appears that Joseph came into Egypt in the reign of Senusret III, an outstanding Middle Kingdom pharaoh. There is a question on the exact time that Joseph was taken to Egypt (1. Senusret III or Sesostris II 1897-1879 B.C.) Jacob's family moves to Egypt about 1876 B.C. **(11)**

H. THE CORRUPTION OF JUDAH'S FAMILY AND CONFIRMATION OF GOD'S CHOICE CHAPTER 38.

1. Genesis Ch.38.

a. It would be good to read chapter 38. It is a bizarre story of events, that seems at first to be a story of Joseph. **However,** it served an important purpose in Genesis of God's **redemption** plan. And also it confirms God's plan of selecting the younger over the elder, despite how others attempted to stop it.

b. <u>**Gen 38:1-5.**</u> **Judah,** who had suggested that the brothers sell Joseph to the Ishmaelites (37:26-27), then **left** for Adullum to stay, (about 15 miles northwest of Hebron) and **married** a **Canaanite** woman. They had three sons, **Er, Onan,** and **Shelah.** This marriage to a Canaanite almost ruined Judah's family. Intermarriage with the Canaanites had been avoided earlier (chap. 34), but not here. This account of living with or mixing with the people of the land helps one understand why God settled His chosen people in the safety of Egypt for its growth.

CHAPTER 5

JOSEPH IN EGYPT

THE RISE OF JOSEPH TO POWER IN EGYPT GENESIS, CH. 39-41.

A. Joseph's temptation by Potiphar's wife, Chap. 39.

1. Gen. 39:1-6a.After the digression in the family history of Judah (chap. 38), which shows that God will use the worst of man to accomplish His purpose, the narrative returns to Joseph who had been taken down to Egypt, and was bought by Potiphar the captain of the guard. We have now reached the point at which the history of the chosen family interweaves itself with the annals of the mighty kingdom of Egypt. It appears that Joseph came into Egypt in the reign of Senusret III, an outstanding Middle Kingdom pharaoh. Joseph had prospered under God and becomes the attendant or steward over Potiphar's household. The property of great men is shown to have been managed by scribes, who exercised most methodical and minute supervision over all the operations of agriculture, gardening, the keeping of livestock and fishing. Every product was carefully registered to check the dishonesty of the laborers, who in Egypt have always been famous in this respect. Joseph's previous knowledge of tending flock, and perhaps of

husbandry, and his truthful character, exactly fitted him for the post of overseer. Joseph's presence was also the means of God's blessing on Potiphar. **(12)**

2. **Gen.39:6-20a.** Joseph was seventeen when he was sold into Egypt, and thirty "when he stood before Pharaoh" (Gen. 41:46). We are not told what portion of these thirteen years he spent in Potiphar's house. Probably not long, as it was his youthful beauty that tempted his master's wife (Gen.39:6-7), whose conduct agrees with the well known profligacy of the Egyptian women. Potiphar's **wife,** shamed or mad by Joseph's refusal to go to bed with her, accuses Joseph of assaulting her. **She** showed to **her household servants,** and then to Potiphar the garment that Joseph left when he fled from her advances. This was the second time Joseph's clothing was used to bring a false report about him (cf. 37:31-33). In both cases he had been serving. But in both cases Joseph ended up in bondage. (v 20)

3. **Joseph** thrived in **prison** by God's favor. As a result, the jailer **put Joseph in charge of** the **prison.** Joseph had thrived in Potiphar's house and was put in charge, and here again he thrived under God's will and was put in charge. Four times, this chapter affirms, **the Lord was with Joseph** (vv. 2-3, 21, 23). Eleven years had passed since Joseph was sold into Egypt, and yet the Divine promise, conveyed in his dreams, seemed farther than ever from fulfillment. **(13)**

B. Joseph's interpretation of the prisoners' dreams Chapter; 40.

1. **Vs. 1-8.** In **prison** two servants of **Pharaoh**—his **chief cupbearer** and his **chief baker**—each **had a** troubling **dream the same night. Joseph** noticed their sadness and agreed to **interpret** their **dreams.**

      a.   He understood their **dreams** to be from **God** (vs. 8) and realized that God was beginning to work His will through dreams and here were two more.

2. **Vs. 9-15. Joseph** interpreted the dreams of the two servants of Pharaoh. **The chief** cupbearer's **dream** had a good interpretation.

3. **Vs. 16-19.** The **dream** of the **baker** was not so good.

4. **Vs. 20-23.** Joseph asked the cupbearer, (v.14) "**But when all goes well with you, remember me and show me kindness; mention me to Pharaoh and get me out of this prison.**" The interpretations proved to be true, for in three days Pharaoh on his birthday restored the cupbearer but executed the baker. Joseph was left in prison, for the cupbearer forgot him, "till after two years, when Pharaoh was disturbed by dreams which none of the scribes or wise men of Egypt could interpret (Gen.,41:8). Then the chief cupbearer remembered his fault and told Pharaoh of Joseph, who was brought out of prison and set before the king.

C. **Joseph's interpretation of Pharaoh's dreams Chapter 41:1-40.**

1. Vs. 1-8, Pharaoh's two dreams troubled him (8), so he sent for all the magicians and wise men of Egypt. "Pharaoh told them his dreams. but no one could interpret them. The cupbearer told the Pharaoh about the Hebrew who interpreted his dream. So the Pharaoh sent for Joseph. God use an Israelite slave to become the wisdom of Egypt. **The magicians** belonged to a political group of experts in handling the ritual books of magic and witchcraft. However, they could not **interpret** Pharaoh's **dreams.** A later group of wise men in Babylon also would be unable to interpret a king's dream, but God would use another Hebrew slave, **Daniel,** to show that

no matter how powerful a nation might be, it is still not beyond God's sovereign control (Dan. 2)

2. **Gen. 41:9-27**, **Joseph** was taken out of prison when the **cupbearer** remembered that **Joseph** interpreted his **dream.** After **Pharaoh** recounted both dreams (41:17-24; cf. vv. 1-8), Joseph explained that **God** was making known **to Pharaoh what He** was **about to do** (vv. 25-27).

3. **Gen. 41:28-32**, Both dreams predicted that **seven years** of plenty would be followed by **seven years of** severe **famine.** Furthermore, Joseph explained that because **the dream** came in **two** versions it signified that it was of **God,** and would be carried out **soon.** Joseph began to understand that God was using him for a great cause by his own two dreams (37:5-7, 9), his two inprisonments (37:36; 39:20). Gen. 41:33-36 God's revelation called for a response. So Joseph advised **Pharaoh** to choose a **wise man** who would oversee storing 20 percent of **the grain** during each of the **years** of plenty for the coming **years of famine. (14)**

4. **Gen.41:37-40**, "**The plan seemed good to Pharaoh and to all his officials. So Pharaoh asked them, "Can we find anyone like this man, one in whom is the spirit of God? (39)" Then Pharaoh said to Joseph, "Since God has made all this known to you, there is no one so discerning and wise as you. (40) "You shall be in charge of my palace, and all my people are to submit to your orders. Only with respect to the throne will I be greater than you."**

   a. Daniel was chosen to be the third highest ruler in Babylon for the same reason (Dan. 5:7, 16). Joseph had been faithful over all the little things God sent him; now he would become ruler over all the land of Egypt under **Pharaoh.**

D. THE EXALTATION OF JOSEPH: Joseph given the position of second in command in Egypt (Genesis 41:41-57)

1. **Vs. 41-46,** The **signet ring** Pharaoh gave **Joseph** was a ring with a seal used for signing documents. When the seal was impressed on a soft clay document which then hardened, it left an indelible impression of the ruler's seal and so carried his authority. Pharaoh also **dressed** Joseph in **linen** clothes and a **gold** neck **chain.** Made him **second in command** to Pharaoh; and **had him ride** in the second **chariot,** before which the people were bidden to fall prostrate, Joseph was to be treated as royal, so all the people could do homage to him. He then gave Joseph a Greek name, Zaphenath—Paaneah, (a revealer of secrets), and gave him Asenath the daughter of Potiphera, a priest, in marriage. Asenath bore him two sons during the seven years of plenty, so that he was not a foreigner ruling Egypt. As a token of the oblivion of his former life, he named his elder son Manasseh (forgetting); and he called the younger Ephraim (double fruitfulness), in grateful commemoration of his blessings,

2. **Vs. 47-52,** Pharaoh's dreams then came true. **The land produced** more crops, so much that it could not be measured. For **seven years Joseph** gathered the crops putting them in storage **in** Egyptian **cities. Joseph** had absolute authority over the food throughout the land. The grain was stored up in each of the cities from the lands of which it was collected; and it was then secured for orderly distribution in the years of famine. When that season arrived, its consumption was guarded by the same policy that had preserved it. The demand was not only from Egypt but for all who had deed? So other countries came into Egypt to buy corn, because the famine was severe in all lands (Gen. 41:56-57).

3. **3.Vs. 53-57,** For **the seven** good **years** were indeed followed by **seven years of** severe **famine,** and **the Egyptians** and people in other **countries** as well went to **buy grain** from the storehouses throughout Egypt. God's revelation to Joseph by dreams was being fulfilled. **(14)**

E. **THE MOVE TO EGYPT (Genesis 42:1-47:27) The settling of Israel in Egypt and becoming a large nation of people.**

1. **THE FIRST VISIT OF THE BROTHERS TO EGYPT (Chapter 42)**

   a. The removal of the chosen family to Egypt was an essential part of the great plan, which God had traced out to their father Abraham. The promise had now been given two hundred years (Gen. 15), and they had neither possessions nor family alliances in the Promised Land. The following events show that God used the famine to bring Israel into Egypt under the rulership of Joseph. The seven years of famine had the most important bearing on the chosen family of Israel. as God had prophesied to Abram (Genesis15:13). Israel could take comfort that in spite of her bondage God would someday enable her to except from Egypt.

   b. **Vs. 1-17,** Because of the famine in Canaan Jacob sent his sons to Egypt to buy food. Recognizing his brothers, **Joseph** would put them to a test by accusing them of being spies. (v.9,12,14) Vs.13, **"But they replied, "Your servants were twelve brothers, the son of one man, who lives in the land of Canaan. The youngest is now with our father, and one is no more"** (They assumed Joseph was dead). **(16) "Send one of your number to get your brother; the rest of you will be kept in prison."** He was handling them harshly (vv. 7, 30), but underneath his harshness there was great affection (ch.45:14). Their presence in Egypt confirmed the truth of his dreams, but not their fulfillment. Joseph knew that all the family must come to Egypt under his ruler ship.

c. **Vs. 29-38,**. Joseph's tests were important in God's plan to bless the seed of Abraham. God planned to bring the family to Egypt so that it would grow there into a great nation. But it was necessary that the people who entered Egypt be faithful to the Lord. It was necessary that the brothers be tested before they could participate in God's blessing. Joseph must test his brothers to see if they are ready for God's work. But one test was not enough; there will be two more. (Chapters 43;44). Now they are ready for the work they are to do.

F. The family moved to Egypt (45:16-47:12)

1. **Ch. 46:1-7**. They must be placed among a people with whom they could not mix, but from whom they might learn the art of civilization and industry. And there, under the discipline of affliction, the family must be consolidated into a nation. Years before, Abram had gone to Egypt during a famine in Canaan (12:10). Now Abram's grandson Jacob and 11 great-grandchildren (not counting Joseph who was already there) were moving there. **God** comforted **Jacob** in his move **to Egypt.** Leaving Hebron (cf. 37:14) his first stop was **Beersheba,** where he sacrificed **to the God of Isaac.** Beersheba was where Isaac had lived and where Jacob left to escape Esau's anger (28:10). Then Jacob received **a vision** from the Lord in the **night. <u>The Lord reiterated the promise that He would make his family a great nation there in Egypt,</u>** and He also stated that He would **bring** that nation **back again.** God had told Isaac not to go to Egypt (26:2), but now He told Jacob **to go.** This vision, which comforted the patriarch, would also encourage the nation

of Israel when Moses would exhort them to leave the land of Egypt and return to Canaan to receive God's promises. **(16)**

G. Jacob blesses his sons and his death, Genesis 49-50.

1. **Vs. 1-2,** In calling his sons to his bedside, Jacob said he would tell them what would become of them in the days ahead. His words to them were deliberately chosen.

   The dying patriarch blessed Joseph and his sons, in the name of the "God, before whom his father, Abraham and Isaac, had walked, the God who had led him all his life, the Angel who had redeemed him from all evil. "Jacob, claimed Ephraim and Manasseh for his own, placing them even before Reuben and Simeon, who by lust and violence had forfeited their birthright; and therefore Ephraim and Simeon were numbered among the head of the tribes of ISRAEL. Jacob ended by giving Joseph an extra portion above his brethren, thus marking him as his heir, and the priesthood was afterwards assigned to Levi. Judah is announced, in a grand burst of prophetic fervor, that of being the ancestor of the Messiah. In fact, the promise, which has been traced step by step, is now centered in this tribe. The key note of the whole blessing is in the meaning of Judah's name, "Praise,' **(16)**

2. Vs.8-10, Judah, note v.10, **"The scepter will not depart from Judah, nor the ruler's staff from between his feet until he comes to whom it belongs and obedience of the nation is his."**

   a. (Jesus Christ)

3. **Vs.18, "Look for your deliverance, O Lord."** Jacob may have been expressing his desire to enjoy the messianic hope, when he would be delivered. (cf. **"redemption"** in Anna's desires; Luke 2:38).

a. Luke 2:38-"**Coming up to them at that very moment, she gave thanks to God and spoke about the child to all who were looking forward to the redemption of Jerusalem.**"

H. The death and burial of Jacob, Genesis 49:29 Ch.50:14.

CHAPTER 6

EXODUS

THE THEME OF EXODUS IS REDEMPTION

A. Exodus Opens with centuries of silence and seeming to Israel that God had forgotten them during the bondage in Egypt. The pride and power of Pharaoh are suddenly broken by a series of miracles, brought by God through Moses. With the deliverance of Israel and the destruction of Egypt, Israel is now a nation born of God. The redeemed people are then led forth to be consecrated at the Mount by ordinances, law and judgments. The Old and New Testament are essentially one-not two covenants but one, gradually unfolding into full perfection, "Jesus Christ Himself being the chief corner stone" of the foundation which is like that of the apostles and prophets. (Eph. 2:20) The Book of Exodus is divided into two sections. The first section (chaps. 1-18) deals with the condition and deliverance of Jacob and his family from the bondage of the Pharaohs Thutmose III and Amenhotep II; the second section (chaps. 19-40) deals with them worshiping God as a nation. It is important that God's adopted people of Israel should have been brought into Egypt, and settled there. Centuries before they struggled to become an independent nation they were continually being influenced by other nations. The early history of Jacob's sons shows the need of their removal from contact with the people of Canaan, and being prepared for the inheriting land that was promised to their fathers. Egypt offered the best, or the only suitable country where the family of Jacob could grow into a nation.

1. **The Nation Promise-Israel, Gen. 32:27-28:cf. Ex. Ch. 19-20. Exodus establishes the fact that the Hebrew nation was the Chosen People of God for the fulfillment of the promise made to Abraham.**

B. **The Deliverance of God's People from Egypt (Exodus chap. 1-18)**

1. Moses described the plight of Israel in Egypt, the rise of a deliverer (himself), and the struggles with Pharaoh's hard heart, which resulted in a miraculous redemption of the nation of Israel through the Sea of Reeds and their safe arrival at Mount Sinai.

   a. Ch. 1-The Israelites Oppressed.
   b. Ch. 2-The birth of Moses and fleeing to Midian.
   c. Ch. 3-4-Moses and the burning bush, signs for Moses and Moses returns to Egypt.
   d. Ch. 5-God promises deliverance from their slavery.
   e. Ch. 6-11 The plagues of God on Egypt and the Passover of the Death Angel and of the crossing over the Sea.

C. THE SETTING: ISRAEL IN EGYPT (EXODUS 1:1-7)

1. The Exodus, or departure of the Israelites from Egypt, closed the 430 years of their pilgrimage. Having learned the discipline of God's chosen family, and having been welded by the hammer of affliction into a nation, they were now called forth under the prophet Moses. Called from the bondage and the sensual pleasures of Egypt to receive the laws of their new state amid the awful solitude of Sinai, Jacob's descendants increased. **"The Israelites were fruitful and multiplied, so that the land was filled with them, (v.6)** (cf. Acts 7:17). The birth of

Moses - Note Num. 26:58-59. **To Amram she borne Aaron, Moses and their sister Miriam."** Had it not been for the command to cast the Hebrew children into the river, Moses would not have been rescued by Pharaoh's daughter, nor trained in all the wisdom of Egypt to fit him for his calling. About 330 years separated Levi from Moses, so that the time from Joseph's death (Gen. 50:26) at the age of a hundred and ten to the growth of the nation as described in Exodus 1:7 was probably little more than 100 years. The adult males in the Exodus totaled 600,000, not counting women and children. (12:37), so the total Israelite population at that time may have been about 2 million.

2. **Vrs,1-5.** These verses provide a connecting link between the patriarchal period described in the last chapters of Genesis and the events in Exodus. God providentially protected the children of **Jacob** (also called **Israel**) and increased their **descendants** from a small group to a large segment of the population in Egypt. Vs. 6-8, Jacob's descendants increased.

D. ISRAEL'S OPPRESSION UNDER THE PHARAOHS (Exodus 1:8-22)

1. Moses discussed two forms of oppression in the reign of a Pharaoh in Egypt's 18th dynasty: slave labor (vv. 8-14) and child extermination (vv. 15-22) God used these practices of the Pharaoh to stir up the people of God to desire deliverance from Egypt.

2. **SLAVERY- Exodus 1:8-14)**

   a. The logic of the new king is stated (vv. 8-10) and also the policy that resulted from his reasoning (vv. 11-14) **"Then a new king, who did not know about Joseph, came to power in Egypt."** If "did not know about Joseph," means, "had no appreciation for

Joseph's character or achievements. **Then** you must remember it has been 430 years that Israel came to Egypt. This Pharaoh voiced two reasons for his concern: the alarming increase in the number of **the Israelites** and the fear of their aligning politically with a foe in time of **war.** So **forced labor** was established throughout the Delta area with Hebrews being required to build the royal **store cities** of **Pithom and Rameses. (Genesis 15;13-14) "Then the Lord said to him (Abram) "Know for certain that your descendants will be strangers in a country not their own, and they will be enslaved and mistreated four hundred years. "But I will punish the nation they serve as slaves, and afterward they will come out with great possessions."** Oppressed (**'ānâh**) is the same word God used in Genesis 15:13 (where it is trans. "mistreated") when He predicted the Egyptian bondage. In spite of the Egyptians' ruthless treatment of **the Israelites,** God prospered them with great numbers. **(17)**

E. THE EXTERMINATION OF CHILDREN (V. 15-22)

1. **Vrs.22, Pharaoh** then enacted an open, more aggressive policy to stem the Israelites' numerical increase. Failing to limit the growth of the people secretively through Hebrew midwives, Pharaoh commanded **his** own **people** to police the decree. So the oppression against the Israelites deepened, but as God's people were suffering under this subjugation, God prepared a deliverer. (Moses)

F. THE DELIVERER OF ISRAEL FROM EGYPT (Exodus Chapters 2-4)

1. The birth of Moses-1580 B.C.

2. World History- 1504 B.C (Thutmose III (Pharaoh of Oppression; 1450 B.C. Amenhotep II Pharaoho of the

Expsus) It traces the historical path of the development of Judah's family into a great nation of two to three million people. It shows God's faithfulness to the covenant He made with Abraham to make his descendants great and to give them a promised land. It sets the stage for an understanding of Christ's work of **redemption** for the human race.

3. Like Moses, he delivers people from bondage.

4. Like the Passover Lamb, he was sacrificed for the sake of sparing people from death.

5. Like Aaron, he is the High Priest of his people.

6. This Exodus, or departure of the Israelites from Egypt, having been humbled through slavery, they are now ready to become a nation for God's work. They were now ready to go forward; under God's protection and are now safe from the bondage of Egypt, to receive the law from God (the 10 Commandments), at the foothill of Mount Sinai.

CHAPTER 7

WANDERING

Period of wandering (From Exodus Ch. 12:37-Ch. 40: Leviticus, Numbers and Deuteronomy)

A. **LEVITICUS** is the expression of God's desire that His holiness be reflected in the life of His chosen people Israel. This is seen in the two phases of Israel's worship and daily walk. (1) The proper way to approach God by Sacrifice (chaps. 1-16) and (b) The proper way to live holy before God by their separation from other nations (chaps. 17-27). Leviticus contains the instructions of God and constituted the basis for civil and religious life among His Chosen People. Leviticus presents the Hebrew nation as a people set apart for the Lord. **(2)** Gives God's plan for consecrating the Israelite nation unto Himself. **(3)** Leviticus 17:11, is the key verse about the significance of blood sacrifice. "For life of a creature is in the blood, and I have given it to you to make atonement for yourselves on the alter. It is the blood that makes atonement for one's life," (4) The blood was a means to "atonement." It signified that a life had been taken in payment for sin and as a substitute for the worshipper's own sin-stained life Cf. Rom. 6:23;

   a. Genesis presents the fall of the race and subsequent promise to Abraham.

    b. Exodus relates the deliverance of Abraham's son Isaac and Jacob whose name was changed to Israel, and Israel's deliverance from their bondage in Egypt.

1. Heb. 10:3-7. "But those sacrifices are an annual reminder of sins, (4) because it is impossible for the blood of bulls and goats to take away sins. (5) therefore, when Christ came into the world, he said; "Sacrifice and offering you did not desire, but a body you prepared for me;

(6) with burnt offerings and sin offerings you were not pleased. (7) Then I said, "Here I am-it is written about me in the scroll. I have come to do your will, O God."

    a. Num.13:1-21:35. Thirty-eight years earlier Joshua had explored Canaan with 11 other spies, only Caleb and Joshua brought back a good report. Because of the people's lack of faith. God sentenced them to forty years in the wilderness, (Num. 13:1-16; there [Num. 13:8] he is called "Hoshea," In whatever way God communicated with Joshua, the message came through clearly. **Moses** died **about (1407 B.C.)**

B. JOSHUA AND JUDGES:

  1. A period of Conquest (Israel in Canaan). (1385-1361 B.C.)

    a. For if God's people are to fill God's will they must have land to fulfill it. Joshua will be God's leader to accomplish it.

    b. The conquest of Canaan lasted about seven years. Caleb was forty years old when he served as a spy in Canaan (Joshua 14:7, Numbers 13:1-6).

    c. The boundaries established by God and **promised** to Abraham (Gen. 15:18-21) and **Moses** (Deut. 1:6-8) were to extend from the wilderness on the south to the **Lebanon** mountain range on the north, and from

the Euphrates River on the east **to the Great Sea,** the Mediterranean, **on the west.**

2. Land promise-Joshua 5:13-12:24-note 1 Kings 4:21.

a. As soon as the mourning for Moses was ended, God appeared to Joshua and commanded him to lead the people over Jordan, with a renewed description of their land as assurance of victory. He commanded them to have courage and to be obedient by meditation of the book of the law, and a promise of God's presence (Joshua 1:1-10). After being assured of the Lord's presence and blessing (Josh. 5:13-15), Joshua began the conquest of Canaan by moving on Jericho and concurring them. This city fell to Israel by the power of God (Josh. 6:1-27).

(1. The nation of Israel is now at home in Canaan.

(1. God has shown His Faithfulness to the covenant (promise) made with Abraham.
(2. God has shown His Wrath against the sinfulness of the Canaanites, and His ability to raise up a leader to see his people through a time of crisis.

b. The closing records of the history of Joshua show us a solemn pause and crisis in the career of Israel. They had now attained that first success which, in their case, was the test of their faithfulness to Jehovah. The capture of Jericho without a fight and the deliverance of the nations of Canaan into their hands. (Joshua 24"13) **"So I gave you a land on which you did not toil and cities you did not build; and live in them and eat from vineyards and olive groves that you did not plant."** Then he reminds them that all they possessed was the gift of God, and not the fruit of their labor. The people were dismissed to their homes. (v.28) Joshua seems to have lived about fifteen years after the final division of the land. Joshua died at the age of 110, (1385 B.C.) Now we shall see how God will fulfill his promise to Abraham that his seed will be a blessing to the world. (Genesis 12:1-4; Gal. 3:6-8,16-18.) **(17)**

3. THE SEED PROMISE:

a. **Prophecies of Christ in the Old Testament, Fulfilled in the New Testament.**

b. Gen. 3:15 ---- Seed of woman, ------------------ Fulfilled Gal. 4:4.

c. Gen. 12:3. ---- Seed of Abraham, ------------------ Matt 1:1; Gal. 3:16.

d. Gen. 17:19 -- Seed of Isaac ---------------------- Luke 3:34.

e. Num. 24:17 - Seed of Jacob --------------------- Mat. 1:2.

f. Gen. 49:10 -- From the tribe of Judah---------- Luke 3:33.

g. Is. 9:7 -------- Heir to the throne of David ----- Luke 1:32.

h. Mic. 5:2------ Born in Bethlehem --------------- Luke 2:4,5,7.

i. Dan. 9:25 ---- Time for His birth ---------------- Luke 2:1,2.

j. Isa. 7:14 ------ To be born of a virgin -------------- Luke 1:26,27,30,31.

k. Jer. 31:15 ---- Slaughter of the innocents ------ Mat. 2:16-18.

l. His. 11:1 ----- Flight to Egypt-------------------- Mat. 2:14, 15.

m. Mal. 3:1------ Preceded by a forerunner-------- Luke 7:24,27.

n. Ps. 2:7-------- Declared the Son of God -------- Mat. 3:17.

o. Isa. 9:1,2----- Galilean ministry ---------------- Mat. 4:13-16.

p. Deut. 18:15 -- A prophet ------------------------ Acts 3:20-22.

q. Isa. 61:1,2 --- To heal the brokenhearted------- Luke 4:18,19.

r. Isa. 53:3 ----- Rejected by his own people----- John 1:11; Luke 23:18.

s. Ps. 110:4----- Priest after order of Melchizedek- Heb. 5:5,6.

t. Zech. 9:9,---- Triumphal entry ------------------ Mark 11:7,9,11.

u. Ps. 41:9 ------ Betrayed by a friend ------------- Luke 22:47,48.

v. Zech. 11:12-- Sold for thirty pieces of silver -- Mat. 26:15.

w. Isa.53:7 ------ Silent to accusations ------------- Mark 15:4,5.

x. Isa. 50:6,----- Spat upon and smitten ----------- Matt. 26:67.

y. Isa. 53:5 ----- Vicarious sacrifice---------------- Rom. 5:6,6,8.

z. Isa. 53:12 ---- Crucified with malefactors------ Mark 15:27,28.

aa. Zech. 12:10 -- Pierced through hands and feet--- John 20:27.

bb. Ps. 69:21----- Given vinegar and gall ---------- Matt. 27:34.

cc. Ps. 22:17,18--Soldiers gambled for his coat --- Matt. 27:35,36.

dd. Ps. 34:20 ----No bones broken --------------------- John 19:32,33,36.

ee. Zech. 12:10; Isa. 53:5---His side pierced --------- John 19:34.

ff. Isa. 53:9 -----Buried with the rich ----------------- Matt. 27:57-60.

gg. Ps. 68:18 ---- His ascension is God right hand ---- Mark 16:19; I Cor. 15:4; Eph. 4:8.

2. God preached the Gospel of good news to Abraham—Gal, 3:6-8, **"Consider Abraham: He believed God, and it was credited to him as righteousness. (7)Understand, then, that those who believed are children of Abraham. (8) The Scripture foresaw that God would justify the Gentiles by faith, and announce the gospel in advance to Abraham." All nations will be blessed through you"**.

CHAPTER 8

PERIOD of JUDGES

FIRST AND SECOND SAMUEL:

A. Samuel, Saul, and David to the birth of Solomon.

B. Before we study First and Second Samuel, we must study Ruth.

1. These four things seem to be the object of the Book of Ruth; **(1)** To present a supplement by way of contrast to the Book of Judges: **(2)** to show the true spirit of Israel; **(3)** to exhibit one of the mysterious connections between Israel and the Gentiles, where by that Israel, at the most critical periods of Israel's history, seems most unexpectedly called in to take a leading part: without knowing, brought the Gentile into Christ's genealogy; **(4)** and to trace the genealogy of David. Not merely an account of the genealogy of Christ, which leads up to Boaz and David, a reminder that Israel's great king, sprang up from the nation of Boaz and Ruth.

2. The story begins with the necessary mention of the time, names, places, and events. The mood was gloom and doom (Cf. Genesis 46, "Jacob goes to Egypt) A man named Elimelech, an Ephrathite of Bethlehem-Judah,

had been driven by a famine into the country of Moab, with his wife Naomi, and their two sons, Mahlon and Chillion.(They must have moved before the boys were 30). The sons married women of Moab, named Orpah and Ruth; and the family lived in that country for ten years. The unfolding of the story revealed how God worked to meet needs of His people, and shows the wisdom of trusting in God and His loving power rather than in Canaanite gods. Bethlehem was about five miles south of Jerusalem. Later Obed, son of Ruth and Boaz, was born in Bethlehem and Obed's grandson David was born in Bethlehem (Ruth 4:18-21; 1 Sam. 17:58). Bethlehem, would also be the birthplace of Jesus Christ, a direct descendent of David. (Luke 2:4-7).

3. Ruth 1:1-2 **"In the days when the judges ruled, there was a famine in the land, and a man from Bethlehem in Judah, together with his wife and two sons, went to live for a while in the country of Moab. (2) The man's name was Elimelech, his wife's name was Naomi, and the names of his two sons were Mahlon and Kilion. They were Ephrathites from Bethlehem, Judah. And they went to Moab and lived there."**

    a. After Naomi husband's death she faced a problem, how long could they live in Moab. But Naomi, though widowed, sorrowing, and in a foreign land, had hope while **her two sons** were still alive. You must remember they are Israelites in a foreign land. Then Naomi's two sons **married Moabite women Orpah** and **Ruth.** The Book of Ruth does not record the length of these marriages but they were childless. Then Naomi's two sons **died. Naomi** had now accumulated a great load of personal grief. **Her husband** and her only **sons** had died before their time. She was a stranger in a foreign land. If the family name were to carry on, there had to be an heir. But having no sons, Naomi **was left without** hope. Her Moabite daughters-in-law offered her no means to an heir. She could offer them no prospect of wedded happiness in her own family, and she wished to convey to them, that no Israelite in his own land would ever wed a daughter of Moab.

4. **Ruth seeking a home- Ch.1:6-18.** Now good tidings reached Moab, **"the Lord had come to the aid of his people by providing food for them"**, the famine was over. Naomi reversed the direction she and her husband had taken. She turned away and headed **back** to **Judah,** her homeland. According to eastern fashion, her daughters-in- law accompanied her on the way. **Naomi,** knowing that the hope of her daughters-in-law to find a husband in Israel would be slight if not impossible, urged them to stay in Moab. Though they were foreigners, they could have married Israelite men for they were under God's covenant.

They needed to be sure to remarry. In the ancient Near East a woman without a husband was in a serious situation because she lacked security, and could starve to death, and widows were especially needy.

5. Ch. 1:8 **Faith** portion now begins. Naomi desired to return home, and in doing so, she had to leave her daughters-in-law in Moab, because she thought that would be best for them. She received a surprise when Ruth said to her, **"But Ruth replied, "Don't urge me to leave you or turn back from you. Where you go I will go and where you stay I will stay. Your people will be my people and your God will be my God. Where you die I will die, and there I will be buried . . .".** (Ruth 1:16-17). Returning with Naomi was a loving choice. Marriage meant security for a woman, and yet Ruth seemed to be giving up this possibility by leaving Moab. Naomi turned away from **Moab** and the errors of the past. She turned her back on the graves of her loved ones and

headed **back** to **Judah,** her homeland. Nothing more is said in the Book of Ruth about Orpah. **Ruth chose to stay with Naomi** and serve her widowed mother-in-law. In Ruth's mind the decision probably meant that she would never have a husband or children. James would have considered her concern for her widowed mother-in-law a religious act (James 1:27). **"Religion that God our Father accepts as pure and faultless is this: to look after orphans and widows in their distress and to keep oneself from being polluted by the world."** Naomi thought she was returning empty-handed, but she had **Ruth the Moabitess** with her. And the harvest was ripe; there was hope. **(20)**

C. Seeking Provisions Ruth meets Boaz (Ruth chap. 2)

a. Vs. 1. They reached Bethlehem at the beginning of barley harvest and Ruth sought subsistence as a gleaner.

What followed turns entirely upon the provisions of the Mosaic law for the "Levirate" marriage of a widow and the redemption of her husband's inheritance by the nearest relative, whose grandfather Nahshon, was prince of the tribe of Judah (I Chron. 2:10). He was a very near kinsman (though not the nearest) to Naomi's deceased husband Elimelech, and consequently to Ruth. As the widow of his son, Ruth went to glean in this man's field. Boaz was visiting the gleaners, not like a grudging farmer, but in the spirit of kindness prescribed by Moses; blessing them, and blessed by them in the name of **Jehovah**. Ruth attracted his attention; and when he learned who she was he asks her to glean only in his field, and commanded the reapers to show her kindness. Boaz knew what she had done, and what she had given up for God. He now assured her, that she would be recompense for the one, and a full reward for the other from Jehovah the God of Israel, under whose wings she had come to trust. And now for the first time, the secret of her sorrow bursts from Ruth, as she tells it to Boaz. "**May I continue to find favor in your eyes my lord, she said, "You have given me comfort and have spoken kindly to your servant, though I do not have the standing of one of your servant girls." (Ruth 2:13**) Boaz was a near relative of Elimelech, Naomi's dead husband (1:2-3; cf. 2:3). Boaz was a man of outstanding qualities. He was a mighty man of valor, capable in his community, and lived a life that was good. **Ruth** understood the rights of the poor in Israel to gather grain in a field after the harvesters had passed through. The corners of the field were to be left for the poor to reap (Lev. 19:9-10; 23:22). Some generous landowners were known to have left as much as one-fourth of their crop for the needy. Naomi encouraged Ruth to go into the fields to gather food for them. Because **Boaz** was already introduced into the story (v. 1), it is clear that Ruth did not **just** happen to be in Boaz's **field.**

She had moved in obedience to her rights in the Law and was guided by God into the Bethlehem field of Boaz.(cf. 2:1) God will later lead the Magi to Bethlehem (Matt. 2:1-8) This fact is important to the unfolding of God's **redemption plan**.

D. **Boaz Marries Ruth (Ch. 4)**

a. Boaz went up to the town of Bethlehem. The town gate was where personal business and civic affairs of the people were transacted. Boaz called together 10 of Bethlehem's elders, and They also sat down. He unfolded the elements in the case step by step. First, he explained that Naomi (and Ruth; cf. v5) had a field for sale that belonged to Naomi's late husband. No information is given as to how she came to possess it. Her poverty apparently required that she sell it. But if possible the land should remain in the family (cf. Jer. 32:6-12). The nearer kinsman had the first right to the property and Boaz was **next** after him.

If Ruth's closer relative would not **redeem** (purchase) it, Boaz was prepared to do so. The man then agreed to **redeem** the piece of land. But then **Boaz** explained that when the nearer kinsman redeemed **the land,** he must also acquire **Ruth the Moabitess.** Apparently at the death of Elimelech the property had passed to Mahlon so Mahlon's **widow** Ruth was included in the redemption responsibility. A son, to whom the property would belong, should be raised up to perpetuate the family **name.** A legal transaction was finalized not by signing a paper but by a dramatic symbolic act that others would witness and remember. The passing of the **sandal** symbolized Boaz's right to walk on the land as his **property** (cf. Deut. 1:36; 11:24; Josh. 1:3; 14:9). After giving his **sandal** to **Boaz,** the unknown **kinsman** moved from the scene and into anonymity. But the name of Boaz has been remembered in all succeeding generations (cf. Ruth 4:14).

b. *An accomplished redemption (4:9-12)* Boaz moved quickly to complete the transaction. He claimed and received the right of redemption, both for Elimelech's land and for Ruth, who was the only widow left capable of giving birth to a son who would perpetuate the family name. **Boaz** called **the elders** to witness the transaction as he took possession of Naomi's **property** and **acquired Ruth the Moabitess** (cf. 1:22; 2:2, 21; 4:5)

c. **Conclusion (4:11-22)** Boaz took Ruth for his wife and she bore him a son, named Obed. It had all been done in God and with God, and the blessing invoked was not withheld. A son would fulfill her heart and bless the family. Naomi now had a "redeemer," not only to support and nourish her but also redeem the family property, and also preserve the name of the family in Israel. And that "redeemer" Boaz whose father was Salmon whose mother was Rahab. Now Boaz the father of Obed whose mother was Ruth, and Obed, the father of Jesse the father of David. **And so Christ, "the son of David," derived his**

lineage from a Moabite woman, who had shown a faith rarely found in Israel, and whose husband was the son of the harlot Rahab, see Ruth 4:17-22; I Chron. 2:10-12; Matt. 1:5; Luke 3:32). **(26) LIBEONIX SIGITAL)**

(1. Point, Jesus' heritage was Jewish and Gentile.

THE MESSAGE OF FIRST SAMUEL!

1. The history of Israel, viewed as the Kingdom of God, consists of three periods: **First,** that under the guidance of Prophets (from Moses to Samuel); **Secondly**, that under the rule of Kings (from Saul to captivity in Babylon); and, **Thirdly**, under the reign of High priests (from Ezra to the birth of Jesus Christ). **The divine guidance had passed through its full development Jesus Christ, the Prophet, King, and High priest of the Kingdom of God.** Together with the second book, it shows the divine origin of the throne of David. This is important not only to Israel's national life but also to the church.(Acts 3:24.) The second book of Samuel takes up the history of David's rise to power and the consolidation of Israel's strength under him, and David's messianic history will become apparent.

THE MESSAGE OF SECOND SAMUEL!

1. First Samuel shows the failure of King Saul; Second Samuel shows the success of King David.

2. Second Samuel shows that God established the house of David.

3. God's promise to 'build a house", for David, 2 Sam. 7:4-16.

4. 2 Samuel 7:16, "Your house and your kingdom will endure forever before me; your throne will be established forever." The New Testament claims ultimate fulfillment

of this prophecy in Christ and the church. Luke 1:1-33, 68-70; Acts 2:29-31; 15:12-18. This prophecy is one of the basic texts from which bring fourth the messianic hope of Israel. The redeemer (Gen. 3:15) The Hebrew term *messiah* (**Gr, christos**) refers to "the anointed one."

5. The two books of Samuel cover a period of growth and development in Israel's history and in the development of the messianic theme of the Old Testament. We will see David's Kingdom reach its greatest glory in Jesus Christ and His church.

6. **"Make us a king, to judge us, like all the nations" (I Sam. 8:5)**

    (1. Samuel applied himself to the resource that never failed him; he prayed to Jehovah (I Sam. 8:6). His indignation was at once justified by assurance. **"They have not rejected thee, but they have rejected Me from reigning over them." (K.J.V.)**

    (2. **The demand for a King, Saul is Anointed King.**

    (3. All nations around had their kings and whether for war or in peace, they wanted a strong hand wielding a central power for the common good. It was always in God's mind to give them a king but in His time frame. It must be admitted that, if ever, circumstances now pointed to this as the proper period for the change. The institution of "Judges," however successful at times and in individuals, had failed as a whole. It had neither given external security or good government to the people. Samuel must soon die; and what after him? Would it not be better to make the change under his direction, instead of leaving the people in charge of two men who could not even keep their hands from taking bribes? Note how Israel was governed through tribes or clans.

CHAPTER 9

KINGS and PSALMS

FIRST AND SECOND KINGS:

The books of Kings began with Israel, a mighty nation under a single righteous king, and ends as two parts of a divided kingdom in captivity and the temple of God in ruins. They wanted not only a king, but royalty like that of the nations around, and for the purpose of outward deliverance; thus forgetting God's dealing in the past, disclaiming simple trust in Him, and disbelieving the sufficiency of His leadership. In fact, they really wanted was a king who wold reflect and embody their idea of royalty, not the ideal which God had set before them. Even with a revelation from God, the need of a Great Redeemer for these people is evident; how much more was there a need by the rest of mankind. **(21)**

1. **Key passages of God's promise to David, (II Sam. 7:12-13.) <u>"When your days are over and you rest with your fathers, I will raise up your offspring to succeed you, who will come from your own body, and I will establish his kingdom (13) He is the one who will build a house for my Name, and I will establish the throne of his kingdom forever."</u>**

    a. Saul's death in (II Sam. 1:1-10) (1010 B.C.) and David be came king. (a). Saul's kingship (1050-1010 B.C.);

David's kingship (1010-970 B.C.); Solomon's kingship (070-930); Division of kinship (930 B.C.); Fall of Israel 721 B.C.)

b. A brief outline of The Reign of David:

(1. Sin with Bathsheba and death of Uriah (II Sam. 11:2-27).

(2. David's repentance (II Sam. 12:1-25, Psalm 51).

(3. David restored as king (II Sam. 19:9-40).

(4. David prepares material for temple (I Chron. 22:1-5).

(5. David's charge to the leaders of Israel (I Chron. 22:17-19).

(6. Solomon appointed king (I Chron. 23:1).

(7. David's last song (II Sam. 23:1-7).

(8. Solomon anointed king (I Kings 2:1-9).

(9. Death of David (I King 2:10-11, I Chron. 29:26-30), (970 B.C.)

THE PSALMS:

1. The conception of God in the book of Psalms:

a. At the heart of the psalms is the personal God of Israel.

(1. The psalmists never tire of praising God as Creator, Sustainer, Lawgiver, Ruler, Vindicator, and Judge.
(2. The personality of God is presented in such a concrete and realistic way.

(3. The psalms stress the infinity of God, Cf. Psa. 139.

    (a. He is omniscient, Vs. 1-6.
    (b. He is omnipresent, Vs. 7-12.
    (c. He is omnipotent, Vs. 13-18.

b. The anticipation of the Messiah (Jesus Christ) in the book of Psalms:

    (1. Both Judaism and Christianity see a number of the psalms as predictions of Christ.
    (2. Note several psalms are cited in the New Testament and interpreted as having spoken of Christ.

        (a. Psa. 2; cf., Acts 4:25-28; 13:33; Heb. 1:5; 5:5.
        (b. Psa. 16; cf. Acts 2:24-31; 13:35-37.
        (c. Psa. 22; cf. Matt. 27:35-46; John 19:23-25; Heb. 2:12.
        (d. Psa. 45:cf. Heb. 1:8-9.
        (e. Psa. 89; cf. Acts 2:30.
        (f. Psa. 110;Cf. Matt. 22:43-45; Acts 2:33-35; Heb. 1:3; 5:6-10; 6L 201 7L 24.

c. Luke 20:42-44 quoting Psa. 110:1-2**, "The Lord says to my Lord; "Sit at my right hand until I make your enemies a footstool for your feet." (2) The Lord will extend your mighty scepter from Zion; you will rule in the midst of your enemies."**

    (1. While most of the Bible is God's voice calling to his creation, Psalms is mankind's voice raised to the Lord. The New Testament writers drew heavily on the Psalms to express many aspects of the person and work of Jesus, the Messiah. As the anointed Davidic King par excellence, Jesus is the great Antitype of the messianic psalms, those psalms that have the king in the foreground. Expositors must exercise caution, however; they must recognize that not all the contents

of messianic psalms apply to Christ (i.e., not all the parts are typological).

(2. Purely prophetic psalms. This category probably applies to Psalm 110, which refers to a future Davidic King who would be the Lord. The New Testament (Matt. 22:44) identifies this King as Jesus Christ, not any other Davidic king. **Eschatological psalms**. Psalms 96-99, the so-called enthronement psalms, among others, describe the coming of the Lord and the consummation of His kingdom. Though they do not refer to a Davidic king, Scripture intimates that they will be fulfilled in the Second Coming of Christ. **Typological-prophetic psalms**. In these psalms the writer describes his own experience with language that goes beyond that experience and becomes historically true in Jesus (e.g., Ps. 22). **Indirectly messianic psalms.** These psalms were written for a contemporary king or for royal activities in general. But their ultimate fulfillment is in Jesus Christ (Pss. 2; 45; 72).

(a. .*Typically messianic psalms.* These psalms are less obviously messianic. The psalmist in some way is a type of Christ (cf. 34:20), but other aspects of the passage do not apply. Certainly the language of the Psalms expresses the hopes and the truths of the faith in a most memorable way, not only as they point to Christ but also as they reflect the struggles of the faithful. **(22)**

CHAPTER 10

ISAIAH

ISAIAH

1. Beginning with Abraham, God called men to speak his will to others through Prophets. The Old Testament prophets were not concerned with founding a new religion but with calling the Jews back to the Law given through Moses. In the context of their work, they not only addressed their immediate situation but also foretold much about the future and the coming Messiah. **The Messiah's** name, "Jesha-yahu" (Heb.) meaning "the salvation of Jehovah". Hezekiah's name which means, "the strength of Jehovah;" and Zedekiah's name, meaning "the righteousness of Jehovah." In this case the name is very appropriate since the salvation of Jehovah is the great theme of the book of Isaiah.

2. The ministry of Isaiah covers the period ca. 740-690 B.C., and the biblical background for his work is found in 2 Kings Chapters 14-20. The first interpreter of O.T. prophecy to indicate that Jesus was, indeed, the object of the O.T. was the message delivered by the angel Gabriel to Zechariah (Luke 1:17a quoting Mal. 4:4-5.)

    a. Luke 1:17—**"And he will go on before the Lord, in the spirit and power of Elijah, to turn the hearts of**

the fathers to their children and the disobedient to the wisdom of the righteous- to make ready a people prepared for the Lord."

b. MALACHI-4:4-5 **"Remember the law of my servant Moses, the decrees and laws I gave him at Horeb for all Israel. (5) See I will send you a prophet Elijah before that great and dreadful day of the Lord comes."**

c. John the Baptist was forerunner of Christ. He preached to thousands and told them to, **"Repent because the kingdom of heaven is near. This is he who was spoken of through the prophet Isaiah; "A voice of one calling in the desert, Prepare the way for the Lord, make straight paths for him" (Matt. 3:2-3.)**

d. Then Gabriel said to Mary (Luke 1:31-33.) **"You will be with child and give birth to a son, and you are to give him the name Jesus. He will be great and will be called the Son of the Most High. The Lord God will give him the throne of his father David, and he will reign over the house of Jacob forever; his kingdom will never end"** Here Gabriel spoke of Jesus' deity. Jesus spoke of this relationship to the Father, and the rulers wanted to stone Him to death for claming to be equal to God.(Jn. 10:29-30)

A. Predictive prophecy:

a. **Isaiah 4:2-6. v2. THE MESSIAH;** 'In that day," is a flashback to chapter 2:3 ". . . in the latter days." Israel and Judah have been punished 2:3 6-4:11 a remnant has escaped; out of that remnant another day (far in the future) a better day, has come. This "branch," has to be, The Messiah (cf. Jer. 23:5; 33:15; Zech. 3:6; 6:12) if the context is to be taken into account. The Branch, Jesus Christ, is to come and demonstrate the true beauty and glory of Israel. The "fruit of the land" probably refers to the Messiah's humanity having its connection to the nation of Israel cf. Num. 13 for "the land of Canaan," which God gave to Israel). The writer of Hebrews probably had this prophecy in mind when he wrote, "For it is evident that our Lord sprang out of Judah . . . Heb. 7:14).

b. **Edward J. Young points to four reasons** *"the fruit of the land" refers to the Messiah; (a) The parallelism between branch and fruit (cf. John 12:24). (b) In many passages of Scripture there is reference to the fruitfulness of the Messianic age. (c) The text provides no contrast between fruitfulness and barrenness; (d) Only when the phrase "fruit of the land" refers to the Messiah is there a satisfactory connection with what follows. It might be, however, that the "fruit of the land" is the product of the Branch, and not the Branch Himself. In this case it would be the redeemed community the church, Christians.* **(ISAIAH Volume 1 by Paul T. Butler Collage Press, Joplin, Missouri; pp.111-112.)**

c. Isa. 44:28 and 45:1- Named Cyrus as the one who would bring Israel out of captivity, and bring about the rebuilding of the temple, about a century and a half before the event. Many messianic prophecies appear in these chapters.

d. Isa. 7:13-14 "**Then Isaiah said, "Hear now, you house of David! Is it not enough to try the patience of men? Will you try the patience of my God also? (14) Therefore the Lord himself will give you a sign: The virgin will be with child and will give birth to a son, and will call him Immanuel."**

(1.(Immanuel-Translates God with you.)

e. In the judgment of author Paul T. Butler of Isaiah volume 1 Collage Press. judgment, the text specifies a "virgin" and is best interpreted as having a single fulfillment in the conception and birth of Jesus Christ.

1) The word in question (Heb. **'almah)** seems always to refer to an unmarried woman. Cf. Gen. 24:43; Ex. 2:8; Psa. 68:25; Prov. 30:19; Song of Sol. 1:3; 6:8.)

2) **Bethulah,** another Hebrew word translated '**maiden**' or **'virgin,'** can refer to a married woman (Joel 1:8); so only **'almah'** could have made it evident that the mother was unmarried.

3) The Septuagint translators (third century B.C.) understood the text to refer to a virgin and translated with a very specific Greek word, **(parthenos).**

4) Isa. 7:14 pointed ultimately to the birth of Jesus as stated in Matt. 1:23.

   (a. Note other passages predicting Jesus, (Luke 1:71 quoting Isa. 11:13-15; Luke 1:76 quoting Isa. 40:2,3; Luke 2:11 alluding to Micah 5;2, Isa. 53:10,12.

   (b. Matthew and Luke are very careful to trace both Mary and Joseph back to the Davidic lineage.

B. The Servant of the Lord in Isaiah.

   a. The section of Isaiah beginning at chapter 35 presents the recurring figure of the Lord. Sometimes the servant is clearly identified with the nation of Israel (Isa. 49:3) and at others is distinguished from that nation (Isa. 49:5-6).The best way to view this material is to see it as you would a pyramid; at the base, the Servant is identified with the entire nation; higher still, there is a narrowing to a faithful remnant; finally, at the summit, the Servant is a single righteous individual. The New Testament applies this material especially chapter 53, to the saving work of Jesus. Acts 8:32-35; Heb. 9:28; I Pet. 2:22-22.

1. **Isaiah's look into the future. Isa. 35:1 through chapter 66:24.**

   a. Chapter 35 finds ultimate fulfillment in the Messianic kingdom (the Church) just as the God-opposing world government was defeated and judged at the crucifixion and resurrection of Christ.

   b. Ch.35:1-7- Isaiah is saying, that in the Messianic age, God's great universal kingdom is to possess the glory of every nation on earth. Christians are urge strongly to cling to the kingdom which cannot be shaken because this was God's goal in the Old Testament. This seems to indicate the writer of the epistle to the Hebrews is saying, the Christian dispensation (or order of things)is the fulfillment of the promises made in Isaiah 35. And "therefore" the messianic age is the point upon which God's people are to focus for "strengthening the weak hands and confirming with the feeble knees." Against the background of the Babylonian exile just predicted, the book looks forward to the Lord's deliverance. In the power of God (40:1-31), heaven would rise up deliverance for the Jews exiled in Babylon through King Cyrus, (41:1-48:22). Beyond restoration to their homeland through Cyrus, the prophet pointed forward to the ultimate **deliverance, which would come through the Suffering Servant (Christ) (49:1-53:12).** The glory that would accompany his great work is anticipated (54:-57:21)

2. **Quotes form O.T. in the N.T. about Jesus Christ in the new age.**

a. In Romans 9:27 Paul quotes Isa. 9:27, **"Isaiah cries out concerning Israel: "Though the number of the Israelites be like the sand by the sea, only the remnant will be saved."** There are other places which state it is a remnant of Israel, which was predicted by the prophets, which would be saved. This remnant we definitely believe is the remnant or group which would obey the Messiah. He then quotes Isa. 1:9 in Rom. 9;29 **WHICH SHOWS US IT WAS A VERY SMALL REMNANT WHICH WAS TO BE SAVED.**

b. Quoting from Isaiah in the New Testament:

(1. Luke 1:32 quoting Isa. 9:7; Dan.2:44; Isa. 2:1-4.
(2. Luke 1:68 quoting Isa. 40:10.
(3. Luke 1:69 quoting Zech. 1:9; Isa. 12:2,3.
(4. Luke 1:71 quoting Isa. 11:13-15.
(5. Luke 1:76 quoting Isa. 40:2,3.
(6. Luke 1:79a quoting Isa. 9:1-3.
(7. Luke 1:79b quoting Isa. 6-9.
(8. Luke 2:10 quoting Isa. 52:7.
(9. Luke 2:11 quoting Isa. 53:10,12; Micah 5:2.
(10. Luke 2:32 quoting Isa. 49:6; 42:6; 60:9.

c. The book closes with pleas for immediate repentance in the part of Isaiah's people (58:1-59:15) and with a realization that things will not be fully right until the **Messiah appears on the scene** (59:16- 66:24). **(23)**

3. **Comfort for God's people, (Isaiah Chap. 40)**

a. <u>Isa. 40:1-2, **"Comfort, comfort my people, says your God. (2) Speak tenderly to Jerusalem, and proclaim to her that her hard service has been completed, that her sin has been paid for, that she has received from the Lord's hand double for all her sins."**</u>

(1. Vs. 1-2 Strengthens that there is definitely a division of Isaiah's book at chapter 40. This, however, does not mean the book has two different authors any more that there were two different authors for the Pentateuch (first five book of the O.T.

Moses, author of the Pentateuch, had different purposes in mind for his books and so used a different style. Isaiah has to use a different style. His main purpose in chapters 40-66 is to preach peace and predict the nature of the future Israel of God, the Church.

(2. **Edward J. Young calls chapters 40-66, "The Salvation and Future blessing of the true Israel of God." These latter chapters are intensely Messianic Isaiah 40:3-4, 6-8; 53:1-12; 55:1-6; 61:1-2 are specifically fulfilled in the N.T.**

(3. If God's covenant people are to be strengthened (comforted) in order to fulfill their messianic destiny they must prepare themselves to receive God's coming to them in the flesh.

b. <u>**Isa. 40:3-5, "A voice of one calling; "In the desert prepare the way for the Lord; make straight in the wilderness a highway for our God. (4) Every valley shall be raised up every mountain and hill made low; the rough ground shall become level, the rugged places a plain. (5) And the glory of the Lord will be revealed, and all mankind together will see it. For the mouth of the Lord has spoken."**</u>

(1. 3-8 **Voice of one calling,** The Hebrew constructing is interesting. Literally it is **(Heb. qol qorea)** "voice, one crying." Each Gospel writer applied Isaiah 40:3 to John the Baptist (Matt. 3:1-4; Mark

1:1-4; Luke 1:76-78; John 1:23). It was John the Baptist who had the climactic job of preparing an immediate nucleus for the coming of God in the flesh, Jesus Christ. It was **John the Baptist who first immersed men and women in water for repentance unto the remission of sins** (Matt. 3:1-2; Mk. 1:4; Lk.3:1-3). John was a **desert** prophet who prepared the way for Jesus Christ, and who **in the wilderness** made **a highway for** Him (cf. Matt. 3:3). Here in Isaiah the entire nation was lost in a spiritual wilderness, and they needed to get ready for a spiritual Kingdom not an earthly kingdom. Though the disciples saw Jesus' glory (John 1:14) in His resurrection and even in His Church, **all mankind** will **see it** at Jesus' Second Coming. (I This. 4:13-18) **(24)**

c. **Isa. 40:6-8, "A voice says, "Cry out." And I said, "What shall I cry? "All men are like grass, and all their glory is like the flowers of the field. (7) The grass withers and the flowers fall, because the breath of the Lord blows on them. Surely the people are grass. (8) The grass withers and the flowers fall, but the word of our God stands forever."**

(1. "A voice says "Cry out." This Voice of verse six is evidently the Lord calling upon His messengers (Christ) to add more to the message of "strengthening". **First,** there is the message to "prepare a way" for the Lord to come. The N.T. applies this to John the Baptist as the one who would prepare the hearts of people to receive the Messiah (Lk. 1:16-17.) **Further** preparation to receive God is proclaiming that we are "all flesh like grass, and all the goodliness that we do is as the flower of the field" Beautiful and good will not last forever in contrast, **God** never fails for

His **Word** endures **forever.** Now the prophets from Isaiah to Malachi were charged to preach man's frailty and his inability to save himself, and the redemption of God provided by grace in some future era. Only the Gospel straightens man out so God can come to Him. The New Testament is the fulfillment of the entire "strengthening "half of Isaiah's prophecy (ch. 40-66)

d. **Isa. 40:9-11, "You who bring good tidings to Zion, go up on a high mountain. You who bring good tidings to Jerusalem, lift up your voice with a shout, lift it up, do not be afraid; say to the towns of Judah, "Here is your God! (10) "See, the Sovereign Lord comes with power, and his arm rules for him. See, his reward is with him, and his recompense accompanies him. (11) He tends his flock like a shepherd: He gathers the lambs in his arms and carries them close to his heart; he gently leads those that have young."**

(1.V.9-11, **GLORIOUS FUTURE**—The construction of the Hebrew in verse nine does not necessitate the "tidings" to be told "to" Zion. Literally translated the verse would read, "So, a mountain high go you to, you bringer of good tiding, Zion." We have indicated this in our paraphrase. In other words, Zion is the bringer of good tiding, not the one to whom good tidings are brought.

Zion and Jerusalem are personified as proclaimer of good news. Isaiah predicted earlier that the law and the word of the Lord would "go "forth" out of Zion and Jerusalem (Isa. 2:3) Isaiah was writing of the glorious future for the benefit of the people of his day. Isaiah's task was to preserve a remnant of faithful Israelites who would be able to endure the disintegration of their nation, go into captivity and return to carry on the Messianic destiny. This remnant was to pass on their faith in the prophetic promises that this destiny would be preserved by God and ultimately fulfilled, if not in their lives, in some glorious era to come.

(2. Vs. 10. What is Zion to proclaim? **(Beho le!** God is coming in mightiness!) **Adpmao-Yaweh, the Lord-Jehovah is coming. Zeroau, arm, usually symbolizes a characteristic-power.** It may also symbolize the Messiah who came as God's "arm" to rule (cf. Isa. 51:4-5; 52:7-10; Luke 1:51. It is apparent that "arm" here and in 52:7-10 refers to the Messiah.

(3. **Note** John 1:6-9; Matt. 3:1-3.

e. Isa. 40:12-17, "Who has measured the waters in the hollow of his hand, or with the breadth of his hand marked off the heavens? Who has held the dust of the earth in a basket, or weighed the mountains on the scales and the hills in a balance? (13) Who has understood the mind of the Lord, or instructed him as his counselor? (14) Whom did the Lord consult to enlighten him, and who taught him the right way? Who was it that taught him knowledge or showed him the path of understanding? (15) Surely the nations are like a drop in a bucket; they are regarded as dust on the scales; he weighs the islands as though they were fine dusts. (16) Lebanon is not sufficient for altar fires, or its animals enough for burnt offerings. (17) Before him all the nations are as nothing; they are regarded by him as worthless and less than nothing."

(1. Who is the God whose coming the prophet has predicted? He is the Sovereign Creator. He has created the earth and its physical features in

perfect proportion necessary to maintain the intricate balance of life.

The fundamental principle of geophysics known as '*isostasy* equal weights' is announced in verse 12. The waters of the earth's surface, the landmass and the atmosphere were created with the preciseness necessary to cause the proper gravitational and hydrological functions to sustain life on the planet. The Hebrew word **SHALISH** is translated **MEASURE** referring to "the dust of the earth . . ." and means literally a THIRD. The surface of the earth consists of land and water. Land, the solid part, covers about 57,584,000 square miles, of about three tenths of the earth's surface. Amazing! How did Isaiah know that "the dust of the earth" was a third 2700 years ago? The only accounting for it is that God revealed it to him. (Isaiah was probably thinking of the Creation account (Gen. 1) in which God spoke and Creation came into being. In irony God had also pointed out to Job by numerous questions that his knowledge was nothing compared with God's (Job 38:2-39:30). The God who is coming is not only omnipotent, He is omniscient. The verb translated **DIRECTED** k.j.v. or **UNDERSTOOD** n.i.v.) in verse 13 is the Hebrew **TIKKEN** and may also be translated **MEASURED.** He who has measured the creation cannot be measured by the creation. He is unmeasurable (cf. Job 5:9; Psa. 145:3; Isa. 55:8-9; Rom. 11:33).

4. GOD'S SOVEREIGN OVER THE WORLD. Isa. 40:21-26,

a. 40:21-22, "Do you not know? Have you not heard? Has it not been told you from the beginning? Have you not understood since the earth was

founded?(22) He sits enthroned above the circle
of the earth, and its people are like grasshoppers.
He stretches out the heavens like a canopy, and
spreads them out like a tent to live in."

(1. God also stretched out the heavens as easy as a
man in Isaiah's day would stretch out a curtain.
These vast, endless, heavens are His dwelling
place. Light travels at approximately 186,000
miles per second. The estimated distance to the
extent of the known universe is 6,000,000 light
years. Multiply the number of seconds in a year
by six million and you get the estimate of the
known universe. But there are areas beyond that,
as controlling history, God establishes rulers and
removes them (cf. Dan. 2:21).

This truth would have been comforting to
Isaiah's original readers who were living under
the threat of the Assyrian Empire and who heard
his prophecy that the Babylonian Empire would
take them into captivity._God, who cannot be
compared to anyone or anything (cf. v. 18) knows
everything about His Creation and sustains it by
His Word (cf. John 1:1-5) **(25)**

5. **The servant of the Lord (Isaiah 42:)**

A. **The Servant and His work (Ch.42:1-17).**

1. **Isa. 42:1-4, "Here is my servant, whom I
uphold, my chosen one in whom I delight; I
will put my Spirit on him and he will bring
justice to the nations. (2) He will not shout or
cry out, or raise his voice in the streets. (3) A
bruise reed he will not break, and a smoldering
wick he will not snuff out. In faithfulness he
will bring forth justice; (4) he will not falter**

or be discouraged till he establishes justice on earth. In his law the islands will put their hope."

a. Verses 1-4 Character of the Servant: The word **(avediy)** is the Hebrew word for bondservant. There is another word, **(sakir),** meaning hired servant. This is the Messiah! That is evident from Matthew 12:17-21. When the Incarnate God came to man, He came as a servant-the lowliest of servants- a slave (cf. Phl. 2:**7 (doulou, Greek for slave) (Bekhiyriy)** means "choice one" and **(ratsethah)** means "willing acceptance" (or "delight"). Of all the servants at Jehovah's disposal, this One was the only acceptable One and so God chose Him. This Servant stands in special relationship to Jehovah. He is the Son (cf. John. 1:18). The Spirit of the Living God upon Him will sustain this Servant He will have God's Spirit without measure (Jn. 3:31-36 and in Him will all the fullness of God dwell (Col. 1:19; 2:9). The Son is the only servant fit to establish the Father's covenant. He will come with all authority and faithfulness of the Father to deliver judgment, **MISHPHAT,** in this instance meaning justice, to the **GOIYM** (Gentiles).

b. **Isa. 42:5-9, "This is what God the Lord says, he who created the heavens and stretched them out, who spread out the earth and all that comes out of it, who gives breath to its people and life to those who walk on it: (6) "I, the Lord, have called you in righteousness; I will take hold of your hand. I will keep you and will make you to be a covenant for the people and a light for the Gentiles, (7) to open eyes that are blind, to free captives from prison and to release from the dungeon those who sit in darkness." (8) "I**

am the Lord; that is my name! I will not give my glory to another or my praise to idols. (9) See, the former things have taken place, and new things I declare; before they spring into being I announce them to you."

(1. Commission of the Servant: God's Servant will come (a) with all the power of the Almighty Creator, (b) in divine righteousness, (c) in divine fellowship, (d) as the covenant of God personified, (e) to deliver, (f) and to fulfill the promises of Jehovah (God) and thus to glorify Him. This Servant will be sent with all the authority and power of Jehovah. He will have creative power resident in Him. He will do the work of the One and only True God.

c. **Isa. 42:10-17, Song of praise to the Lord,**

d. **Isa. 42:18-25, Israel's current blind and deaf condition.**

6. **ISRAEL'S ONLY SAVIOR, (Isaiah chapters 43:1-Ch.44:5)**

A. **To be a possession-Isaiah Cha. 43:1-21**

a. Isa. 43:1-7. **"But now, this is what the Lords says, "he who created you, O Jacob, he who formed you, O Israel: "Fear not, for I have redeemed you; I have summoned you by name; you are mine. (2) When you pass through the waters, I will be with you; and when you pass through the rivers, they will not sweep over you. When you walk through the fire, you will not be burned; the flames will not set you ablaze.**

(3) For I am the Lard, your God, the Holy One of Israel, your Savior; I give Egypt for your ransom, Cush and Seba in your stead. (4) Since you are precious and honored in my sight, and because I love you, I will give men in exchange for you, and people in exchange for your life. (5) Do not be afraid, for I am with you; I will bring your children from the east and gather you from the west. (6) I will say to the north, "Give them up! And to the south, 'Do not hold them back.' Bring my sons from afar and my daughters from the ends of the earth-(7) everyone who is called by my name, whom I created for my glory, whom I formed and made."

(1. **Verses 1-4** This chapter tells the very reason of God's purpose to establish Israel's servanthood, **"redemption."** This whole section of salvation through God's servant (chapters 40-53), is an overall view of the relationship of Israel and the Messiah. Israel was called for the messianic purpose, but she sinned. The captivity, which was certain to come, was symbolic of the strained relationship between Israel and God. Israel willfully and deliberately separated themselves from God. (cf. Isa. 30:1-14 etc). The separation was not God's choosing. However, in order to demonstrate Israel's need for God's holy fellowship, God delivered her to captivity.

(2. **Verse seven** indicates that God is referring to His spiritual people not just physical Israel, when it says, "every one that is called by my name." Jesus made plain who God's sons were in John 8. Not all descended from Israel belong to Israel (cf. Rom.2:25-29;, 9:6; Gal. 6:13-16, etc). Anyone who does not come to God through Jesus Christ is not called by God's name. The arrangement of

the word, **CREATED, FORMED and MADE**, seem to be the work of God in the redemption of those called by His name. Two words are used in verse one to emphasize Jehovah's claim upon Israel; **"bara,** create and **yatzar,** form, shape, are the distinctive Hebrew words showing God's unique relationship to Israel. She is His possession by right of His having brought her into existence and having molded her into what He wants her to be.

The Hebrew word for redeemed is **goael** and a derivative of the same word is sometimes translated kinsman (cf. Ruth. 3:2). Israel is God's precious possession. First there is the new creation (the initial new birth, becoming a Christian), then the **SHAPING or MOLDING** of that life into the image of Christ and last, the **PERFECTION and fitting** work of glorifying the child of God. Isaiah is talking about regeneration. He is saying that being an Israelite was in name only.

B. To be a Proclaimer-Isaiah 43:8-13

a. Verses 8-13 **"Lead out those who have eyes but are blind, who have ears but are deaf. (9) All the nations gather together and the peoples assemble. Which of them foretold this and proclaimed to us the former things? Let them bring in their witnesses to prove they were right, so that others may hear and say, "It is true." (10) "You are my witnesses," declares the Lord, and my servant whom I have chosen, so that you may know and believe me and understand that I am he. Before me no god was formed, nor will there be one after me. (11) I, even I, am the Lord and apart from me there is no savior. (12) I have revealed and saved and proclaimed- I, and not some foreign god among you. You are my witnesses," declares the Lord, "that I**

am God. (13) Yes, and from ancient days I am he. No one can deliver out of my hand. When I act, who can reverse it?"

(1. Vs.8-10- **MESSENGER:** The god of Israel is the only true God. He alone has the truth He alone knows righteousness and holiness. Israel is to be the only "messenger" of truth and righteousness, (cf. Ex. 19:5; Deut. 4:6-7, 14:2; 26:18; Psa. 135; Deut. 7:6). The passage before us deals with God's call to this servanthood. Israel had to fulfill her purpose (cf. Amos 3:9-11; Jer. 2:9-13; 18:12). They were to have witness of the message, but rejected this for false gods, (cf. Amos 3:9-11; Jer. 2:9-13; 18:13)." She was given the land of Canaan to show the worldly nations that Israel was God's chosen people. But she became as unholy and worldly as the other nation! Now Isaiah is calling for a remnant of Israel to turn again to God's holy purpose.

Israel is not called to be a mighty worldly power dominating other nations and exercising world power. **Israel was to point the way to new Israel, the church.** Israel testified by her very existence and was called to testify by her deeds and words that Jehovah is the only God.

(2. **Vs. 11-13 MESSAGE**: The absolute sovereignty of Jehovah is the message Israel is to proclaim. They are witnesses to it. They have seen and heard first hand, for that is what a witness is. A witness does not tell what he thinks or feels, he tells what he has seen and heard. Therefore, Israel must be God's witness. God has not shown Himself to any other people so overwhelmingly, and extensively. God has no other witnesses. Isaiah was in the temple, God asked, "Who will go for us, whom shall I send?" (cf. Isa. 6) There cannot be another witness and there cannot

be another God. There is only one God. He is from everlasting to everlasting. **(26)**

7. God's Mercy and Israel's Unfaithfulness-Isaiah 43:14-28.

A. Vs. 14-17- **OPPRESSOR DEFEATED**.

a. **ISAIAH 43:18-21 OPRESSED DELIVERED: (18) "Forget the former things; do not dwell on the past. (19) "See, I am doing a new thing! Now it springs up; do you not perceive it? I am making a way in the desert and streams in the wasteland. (20) The wild animals honor me, the jackals and the owls, because I provide water in the desert and streams in the wasteland, to give drink to my people, my chosen, (21) the people I formed for myself that they may proclaim my praise."**

(1. **V. 18-21,** But, as grand and glorious as these great national deliverance's are, they are warned they should not let their hopes rest on them. God is going to do a new thing much more glorious. The "new" thing is apparently not just the deliverance from the Babylonian captivity, though that is its starting place.

It must be more than that for the deliverance from captivity is not any more glorious than the exodus from Egypt. The "new" thing in itself is the wondrous new redemption in the death and resurrection of the Messiah (cf. Isa. 42:9-10; 48;6; 62:2; 65:17; 66:22; Ezk. 11:9; 18:31, the new thing God is going to do in the messianic kingdom. God, who in the first Exodus brought Israel out of Egypt, would do it again. Still there will be a third and final "Exodus" that will take place when the Messiah returns to gather His people (cf. 43:5-6) in His Church, the true seed of Abraham. (1. Note Gal. 3:26-29; and Gal. 3:16.

(2. Isaiah 43:22-28: Israel was called to praise and exalt the name of Jehovah by worshiping Him and keeping His commandments. However Israel did not obey Jehovah' law. They simply forgot God and were living in the present, not remembering the past or looking to the future, and their **sins** had wearied **God! (cf. Mal. 2:17) "You have wearied the Lord with your words. "How have we wearied Him?" you ask. By saying, "All who do evil are good in the eyes of the Lord, and he is pleased with them" or "Where is the God of justice?"**.

8. **THE POWER OF THE LORD'S SERVANT-Isaiah ch. 44-49**

A. **Sovereign over all gods, -Chapter 44.**

B. **Shows favor to the faithful-ch. 44:1-8.**

a. Isaiah 44:1-5 **"But now listen, O Jacob, my servant, Israel, whom I have chosen. (2) This is what the Lord says, he who made you, who formed you in the womb, and who will help you: Do not be afraid, O Jacob, my servant, Jeshurun, whom I have chosen. (3) For I will pour water on the thirsty land, and streams on the dry ground; I will pour out my Spirit on your offspring, and my blessing on your descendants. (4) They will spring up like grass in a meadow, like poplar trees by flowing streams. One will say, 'I belong to the Lord; another will call himself by the name of Jacob; still another will write on his hand, "The Lord's and will take the name Israel."**

(1. Vs.1-2: Invigorates (encourages). Although the chastening judgment of Jehovah is predicted with absolute certainty (ch. 43) upon Israel, still Israel is the chosen of the Lord.

(2. Vs3-5: **THE PROPHET**: Suddenly makes a dramatic shortening of the remnant of Israel formed from the chastening captivity, Isaiah focuses his prophetic telescope down on the time when God will "pour my Spirit upon your seed (K.J.V.)_and your offspring." God's redemptive purpose will be accomplished through the "seed" and "offspring" of Israel._What is the pouring out of the Spirit? Is it the special, miraculous Spirit on the apostles at Pentecost (cf. Joel 2:28f; Acts 2:14f), or is it the promise of the Holy Spirit to all obedient believers (Isa. 32:14 ; Acts 2:38-39) Isaiah could be making a general prophecy in which both the seed and Israel were intended since without the revelation of the gospel of salvation through the Spirit to the apostles at Pentecost (Acts 2:16-21) there would not have been the indwelling of the Spirit. Whatever the case may be, I feel certain Isaiah's prophecy of the Spirit here is intended to be fulfilled with the new covenant (Church) believer._Christ is the "seed" and "offspring" (cf. Gal. 3:15-29) and Christians are "offspring" by being in Him. Gentiles will take pride in belonging to Jehovah. Nothing short of conversion and rebirth could fulfill this prophecy! **(Isaiah III, by Paul T. Butler, College Press, Joplin, Missouri, Third printing 1990)** (27)

9. **Isaiah 44:6-23 "WORSHIP THE LORD NOT IDOLS.**

A. SOVEREIGN IN SALVATION-Isaiah. 45

1. **OMNIPOTENCE**: (Having unlimited authority) Isaiah **45:1-8.** "**This is what the Lord says to his anointed, to Cyrus, whose right hand I take hold of to subdue nations before him and to strip kings of their armor, to open doors before him so that gates will not be shut: (2) I will go before you and will level the mountains. I will break down gates of bronze and cut through bars of iron.**

(3) I will give you the treasures of darkness, riches stored in secret places, so that you may know that I am the Lord, the God of Israel, who summons you by name. (4) For the sake of Jacob my servant, of Israel my chosen, I summon you by name and bestow on you a title of honor, though you do not acknowledge me. (5) I am the Lord, and there is no other; apart from me there is no God. I will strengthen you, though you have not acknowledged me, (6) so that from the rising of the sun to the place of its setting men may know there is none other beside me. I am the Lord, and there is no other. (7) I form the light and create darkness, I bring prosperity and create disaster; I, the Lord, do all these things. (8) You heavens above, rain down righteousness; let the clouds shower it down. Let the earth open wide, let salvation spring up, let righteousness grow with it; I, the Lord, have created it."

(**1. Vs.**1-4 **ANOINTED**: The word translated **ANOINTED** is the Hebrew word **MESJIKLO,** form of the word **MESSIAH.** It is amazing to learn that God has "anointed" a pagan emperor to become a "messiah" for His people. Yet the Lord has used many "servants" from among the heathens (world), such as Rahab who saved the spies in Jericho (Joshua 2:) (see Daniel 7:8,

Jer. 37:1-11) to fulfill His redemptive plan. It is apparent that Cyrus, in his deliverance of Israel, served as **a type** of the Messiah-Servant to come, Jesus Christ. Cyrus was born in a little province in north-western Elam and just south of Media. For more than a hundred years after this prophecy. Cyrus freed Israel from their Babylon bondage as Christ freed man- kind from the bondage of sin.

(2. **Types of Messiah in O.T.** Jesus set great value upon types. Again and again He referred to them and showed how they pointed to Himself. Manna from heaven; Jonah's death and resurrection from the whale; Light of the World; etc. The very high place that is accorded types by writers of the N.T, show their importance (Hebrews, Romans, Gospel of John, Revelation). The Epistle to the Hebrews is almost entirely made up of references to the O.T. The O.T. is the shadow-Christ is the substance.

(3. Vs.5-8, **ALMIGHTY**: This is one of the passages of the Bible teaching that God is personally involved in His creation. God has not created the universe and wound it like a clock, only to go off somewhere and let it run itself. He is personally and directly involved in its continued operations.

(a. In Christ all things consist, or hold together, Col. 1:17.
(b. He upholds all things by the word of His power, Heb. 1:3.
(c. He makes his sun rise on the evil and on the good, Nt. 5:45.
(d. His wrath is revealed from heaven, Rom. 18:32, "In the things that have been made."

B. **OBEDIENCE: Ch. 45:9:13.**

C. **ORDER: Ch. 45:14:19.**

D. **SOVEREIGN OVER NATIONS. Isaiah 46-47.**

    (1. Condemning their gods. Ch. 46:1-13.
    (2. Conquering their governments, Ch. 47:1-15.

10. **SOVEREIGN IN WISDOM, Isaiah 48.**

    a. **Proof. Ch.48:1-8.**
    b. **Perspective, Ch.48:9-16.**
    c. **Practice, Ch. 48:17-22.**

11. **The Servant of the Lord delivers "God's people" Isaiah Ch. 49-66.**

    a. **PROGRAM OF THE LORD'S SERVANT-Isaiah Chapters. 49-53.**
    b. **Rescue, Ch. 49.**
    c. **DESPISED SERVANT 49:1-6.**

        (1. DESPISED SERVANT—Isa. 49:1-6 <u>"Listen to me, you islands; hear this, you distant nations: Before I was born the Lord called me; from my birth he has made mention of my name. (2) He made my mouth like a sharpened sword, in the shadow of his hand he hid me; he made me into a polished arrow and concealed me in his quiver. (3) He said to me, "You are my servant, Israel, in whom I will display my splendor."</u>

        <u>(4) But I said, "I have labored to no purpose, I have spent my strength in vain and for nothing. Yet what is due me is in the Lord's hand, and my reward is with my God." (5) And now the Lord says, he who formed me in the womb to be his</u>

servant to bring Jacob back to him and gather Israel to himself, for I am honored in the eyes of the Lord and my God has been my strength, (6) he says: "It is too small a thing for you to be my servant to restore the tribes of Jacob and bring back those of Israel I have kept. I will also make you a light for the Gentiles, that you may bring my salvation to the ends of the earth."

(a. From this point on, Babylon and Cyrus are not directly mentioned. The Messiah-Servant and the glory of His future kingdom will be pre-eminent to everything the prophet has to say to his people, in relationship to the future messianic Servant (Jesus). Note the following: Called from the womb (he is to be born of a woman) Isa. 7:14; 9:6; Micah 5:2,)

(1. Named while still in the womb, (Mt. 2:18-25; Lk. 1:30-35; Isa. 7:14; 9L6,)

(2. His mouth a "sharp sword" Rev. 1:16; 2:12; Heb. 4:12).

(3. He is called "Israel" (Prince of God) Isa. 9:6; Dan. 9:24-27; Lk. 1:30-35.)

(4. Jehovah is to be glorified in Him (cf. Jn. 12:27-36; 17:1-5.

(5. He is to be a light to the Gentiles (Isa. 9;1-2; Mt. 4:12-17; Lk. 2:29-32; Isa.42:6.
(6. He is Jehovah's salvation to the end of the earth.

(7. The Servant is a "polished arrow" and His words are a sharp sword. The Servant is kept in Jehovah's "quiver" until the proper time for battle.

(8. The Hebrew word **YISERAEL** means "Prince of God." Jesus was descended from David according to the flesh (Rom. 1:1-6), and promised the throne of His earthly father and His Heavenly Father, therefore, Prince (cf. Isa. 9:6; Dan. 24:27; Lk. 1:30-35, etrc.)

12. DESIRABLE SAVIOUR: The Servant of the Lord: Isaiah 49:7-13.

a. Vs. 7-13 <u>"This is what the Lord says, the Redeemer and Holy One of Israel, to him who was despised and abhorred by nation, to the servant of rulers; "Kings will see you and rise up, princes will see and bow down, because of the Lord, who is faithful, the Holy One of Israel, who has chosen you. (8) "This is what the Lord says: "In the time of my favor I will answer you, and in the day of salvation I will help you; I will keep you and will make you to be a covenant for the people, to restore the land and to reassign its desolate inheritances, (9) to say to the captives, 'Come out,' and to those in darkness, 'Be free!'" They will feed beside the roads and find pasture on every barren hill. (10) They will neither hunger nor thirst, nor will the desert heat or the sun beat upon then. He who has compassion on them will guide them and lead them beside springs of water. (11) I will turn all my mountains into roads, and my highways will be raised up. (12) See, they will come from afar, some from the north, some from the west, some from the region of Aswan. (13) Shout for joy, O Heavens; rejoice, O earth; burst into song, O mountains! For the Lord comforts his people and will have compassion on his afflicted ones."</u>

(1. Vs. 7-8 **Vindication (Restoration):** Jehovah calls Himself "Redeemer of Israel." Redeemer is the Hebrew word, **(go'el,)** which means, avenger,

vindicator, ransomer, retributor, recoverer. Jehovah is going to redeem mankind through His Servant, and when He does His Servant will be vindicated. Why is the Servant here called **Israel?** This cannot refer to the nation because the Servant is to draw that nation back to God. The Messiah is called Israel because He fulfills what Israel should have done.

In His person and work He is the fulfillment of Jehovah's (God) covenant with Abraham and his spiritual descendants, and is not to be understood literally. We come into covenant relationship with God by being "joined" in discipleship to Jesus. Disciples of Jesus are those who have been baptized into Him and keep his word (Mt. 28:18f; Jn. 8:31f). Furthermore the Servant will shepherd Jehovah's people (see Isa. 40:11; John 10:11.) The Servant will change everything! The Servant people will not be in want (Psa. 23); when they hunger or thirst after righteousness, they will be filled (Mt. 5:6). Isaiah called in Vs. 8, "**the time of God's favor the day of salvation,**" The Lord will enable the Servant (Isa. 42:6, "**to be a covenant for the people**") to fulfill God's covenant promises to Israel. **The New Israel, the church**. (28)

13. DEJECTED ZION: Isa. 49:14-21,

a. **(14. "But Zion said, "The Lord has forsaken me, the Lord has forgotten me. "(15) Can a mother forget the baby at her breast and have no compassion on the child she has borne? Though she may forget, I will not forget you! (16) See, I have engraved you on the plams of my hands; your walls are ever before me. (17) Your sons hasten back, and those who laid you waste depart from you. (18) Lift up your eyes and look around; all your sons gather and come to you. As surely as I live, "declares the Lord, "You will**

wear them all as ornaments; you will put them on, like a bride. (19) Though you were ruined and made desolate and your land laid waste, now you will be too small for your people, and those who devoured you will be far away. (20) The children born during your bereavement will yet say in your hearing, "This place is too small for us; give us more space to live in. (21) Then you will say in your heart, 'Who bore me these? "I was bereaved and barren; I was exiled and rejected. Who brought these up? I was left all alone, but these, where have they come from?"

(1. V. 14-18; The people of Zion are represented as being in a state of deep despondence. This is anticipating the nation of Judah in exile in Babylon.

The Psalmist of the exile wrote; "By the rivers of Babylon, there we sat down, yea, we wept, when we remembered Zion . . ." (see Psa. 137:1f,) Whatever God dreams or envisions comes to pass. God's dreams are not sand-castles. He has proven this through dreams and visions He manifested to the world by the instrumentality of His prophets they all come to pass! So when God envisions the walls of Zion built forever, they shall be built forever! Maybe not in the lifetime of Isaiah, or the returned exiles, but when the messiah arrives, He shall build the eternal walls of Zion (cf. Heb. 12:25-28,) "a kingdom that cannot be shaken" is already being received by the recipient of the Hebrew epistle. Whenever Isaiah refers to Zion he is referring to the city of David (Jerusalem) and now Jerusalem is the church. Jehovah swears by His own life (which is, of course, never ending and absolute).

14. God will call on the Gentiles, Isaiah 49:22-26.

a. v. 22-26: "This is what the Sovereign Lord says; "See, I will beckon to the Gentiles, I will lift up my banner

to the peoples; they will bring your sons in their arms and carry your daughters on their shoulders. (23) Kings will be your foster fathers, and their queens your nursing mothers. They will bow down before you with their faces to the ground; they will lick the dust at your feet. Then you will know that I am the Lord; those who hope in me will not be disappointed." (24) Can plunder be taken from warriors, or captives rescued from the fierce? (25) But this is what the Lord says; "Yes, captives will be taken from warriors, and plunder retrieved from the fierce; I will contend with those who contend with you, and your children I will save. (26) I will make your oppressors eat their own flesh; they will be drunk on their own blood, as with wine. Then all mankind will know that I, the Lord, am your Savior, your Redeemer, the Mighty One of Jacob."

(1. V. 22-23 Two different Hebrew words are used to denominate the recipients of Jehovah's **"ensign"**-goim (Gentiles, or nations) and **"ammim** people. Gidlestone says," . . . . the word **goim** primarily signifies those nations, which lived in the immediate neighborhood of the Jewish people. They were regarded as enemies, as ignorant of the truth, and sometimes as tyrants.

"You have made me the head of the heathen "**giom**"; a people **"am"** whom I have not known shall serve me. "This will come to pass when Jehovah shall be acknowledged as holding rule as King of the **'goim'**" (Jer. 10;7; Hos. 1:9-10; 2:23). This by-play upon the words "**goim and ammim**" in verse 22 seems to indicate the delivered society referred to, although it may begin with deliverance from exile by Cyrus, and its ultimate goal as the messianic society (the Church).

(a. Ensign and goim=Gentiles or nations.

(b. Ammim=people

(2. <u>Vs.24-26, When Israel returns to the land in the future the Gentiles</u> will worship before **the Lord** and will be friendly toward Israel. In fact the Gentiles will even help transport Israelites to Palestine. Cyrus (Heb. **KORES**, Old Persian (**KURUS**) the king of Persia whom Isaiah foresaw as responsible for the restoration of the Temple at Jerusalem and as the 'Messiah' delivered the Jews from exile in Babylon. Cyrus allows first captives deportation under Zerubbabel in 536 B.C. And work begins on second temple in 535 B.C. it is completed in 515 B.C. He was an instrument of God's plan for His people. The Gentile leaders will be subservient to Israel, which will cause her to realize that **the Lord** really is in control of the world (v. 23). **(29)**

15. <u>Israel warning to walk by faith—Isaiah Ch. 50.</u>

a. **OBEDIENT CHRIST;** Isaiah 50:1-9: Israel has accused Jehovah of casting her off, "illegally" or without justification. The actual facts are quite different. Many times Jehovah came to Israel (Through prophets and providential judgments) to rescue her from her deliberant plunge into worldly pagan slavery, but her ears were closed to God's call. The actual facts are that God demonstrated that He not only wanted to save Israel from enslavement but He had the power to save her.

Time and time again He came, but they would not listen. In fact, he was rejected (cf. Isa. 30:8-11), until in the fullness of time He came incarnate to His own and they crucified Him! Delitzsch interprets these as the words of the Servant. Certainly Isa.50:4ff. would seem to be an apparent reference to the Red Sea exodus (. . ."at my rebuke I dry up the sea . . .") and would indicate these to be the words of Jehovah since Jehovah and the Servant are One (Jn. 1:1-8; 14:8-11; Col. 1:19; 2:9). Furthermore, Jehovah (God) will give the Servant divine assistance.

The Servant's secret is godly faith and dependence (cf. Heb. 5:7) that Jehovah will, in his own good time, turn the Servant's humiliation into glory. (cf. Acts 1:1-11)

   b. **Vs. 10-11: STRENGTH:** Israel is offered two options in relation to **Jehovah's prediction of the coming Servant**. The outcome depends on one's attitude toward Jehovah's coming servant. Parenthetically, it may be well to point out here that the "Servant" cannot possibly be the nation Israel since fearing the Lord and hearkening to the voice of the Servant are synonymous. Hearkening to human Israel (even the best of Israel) cannot be seriously equated with fearing Jehovah. By "obeying" the voice of the Servant is meant believing, accepting and obeying the predictions of the coming Servant in so far as their limited revelation of God's will at that time would direct them in such obedience. Israel must believe that God's redemptive purposes were to be fulfilled in a coming "suffering Christ" (I Pet. 1:10-12) and prepare themselves to be used by Jehovah as the instrument of the coming by obeying God's instructions for them. **(30)**

16. The remnant to be exalted Isaiah 51:1-52:12.

   a. **The Lord's comfort of the remnant, 51:1-16.**

   b. **Turn to justice. 51:1-8.**

     (1. 51:1-8 "Listen to me, you who pursue righteousness and who seek the Lord; Look to the rock from which you were cut and to the quarry from which you were hewn; (2) Look to Abraham, your father, and to Sarah, who gave you birth. When I called him he was but one, and I blessed him and made him many. (3) The Lord will surely comfort Zion and will look with compassion on all her ruins; he will make her deserts like Edon, her wasteland like the garden of the Lord. Joy and gladness will

be found in her, thanksgiving and the sound of singing.

(4) "Listen to me my people; hear me, my nation: The law will go out from me; my justice will become a light to the nations. (5) My righteousness draws near speedily, my salvation is on the way, and my arm will bring justice to the nations. The islands will look to me and wait in hope for my arm. (6) Lift up your eyes to the heavens, look at the earth beneath; the heavens will vanish like smoke, the earth will wear out like a garment and its inhabitants die like flies. But my salvation will last forever, my righteousness will never fail. (7) Hear me, you who know what is right you people who have my law in your hearts: Do not fear the reproach of men or be terrified by their insults. (8) For the moth will eat them up like a garment; the worm will devour them like wool. But my righteousness will last forever, my salvation through all generations."

(1. **Established, v.1-5:** This chapter predicts the coming of Jehovah's rule of justice through His law. It is, of course, an integral part of the whole section discussing Salvation through God's Servant (ch. 40-53). The Lord's justice over Israel will extend over the whole world.

(2. **Vs. 6-8,** It is the will of God concerning redemption through the Servant (cf. Isa. 42:1-3), the Servants law. That this law (or will) of God concerning future salvation through an atoning Servant was written on the hearts of some before Christ was born is evidenced by Abraham rejoicing to see Christ's day (Jh. 8:56). And Isaiah seeing the glory of the Christ (42:1-4), the prophets inquiring about Him (I Pet. 1:10-12.) and from all the

faithful in Hebrews, chapter 11. The prophecy in Jeremiah 31:31-34 does not exclude every Jew of the Old Testament dispensation from the capacity to have God's law written on their heart through faith. (cf. Heb. 11ch.) **(31)**

17. **TRUST IN JEHOVAH: Ch. 51:12-16.**

   a. **The Lord's comfort of Jerusalem, 51:17-52:10.**

   b. **Tormentors judged, 51:17-23.**

18. **SALVATION Isaiah 52.**

   a. **Redemption; Ch. 52:1-6.**

   b. **v.1-6: "Awake, awake, O Zion, clothe yourself with strength. Put on your garments of splendor O Jerusalem, the holy city. The uncircumcised and defiled will not enter you again. (2) Shake off your dust; rise up, sit enthroned, O Jerusalem. Free yourself from the chains on your neck, O captive Daughter of Zion.**

   (3) For this is what the Lord says:" You were sold for nothing, and without money you will be redeemed." (4) For this is what the Sovereign Lord says: "At first my people went down to Egypt to live; lately, Assyria has oppressed them. (5)And now what do I have here? Declares the Lord. "For my people have been taken away for nothing, and those who rule them mock, declares the lord. And all day long my name is constantly blasphemed. (6) Therefore my people will know my name; therefore in that day they will know that it is I who foretold it. Yes, it is I".

   (1. Ch. 52:1-2. **DISSOCIATION FROM PAGANISM:** As before, the Prophet is speaking of the future

Babylonian exile in the present tense. He is directing the exhortation to his small band of disciples (the "remnant") which shall form the nucleus of "Zion". This remnant must prepare itself for imminent exile into Babylon. It must strengthen itself by believing what Isaiah is predicting about its Messiah and its messianic role. Zion must commit itself to an adornment of holiness so that when they go into captivity they will be able to keep themselves separated from the filth and enslavement of heathenism with which it will be so alluringly surrounded.

19. Ch. 52:3-12, **DELIVERANCE FROM PERSECUTION: (PEACE)**

   a. **Redeemed-3-6.**

   b. **Peace-7-12**

   (1. **Isaiah 52:7-12-"How beautiful on the mountains are the feet of those who bring good news, who proclaim peace, who brings good tidings, who proclaim salvation, who say to Zion, "Your God Reigns!" (8) Listen! Your watchmen lift up their voice; together they shout for joy. When the Lord returns to Zion, they will see it with their own eyes. (9) Burst into songs of joy together, you ruins of Jerusalem, for the Lord has comforted his people, he has redeemed Jerusalem. (10) The Lord will lay bare his holy arm in the sight of all the nations, and all the ends of the earth will see the salvation of our God. (11) Depart, depart, go out from there! Touch no unclean thing! Come out from it and be pure, you who carry the vessels of the Lord. (12) But you will not leave in haste or go in flighr; for the Lord will go before you, the God of Israel will be your rear guard."**

(1. Vs. 7-10; Apparently we have in this prediction of Isaiah an instance of "shortened perspective." That is, the prophet is predicting the deliverance of Judah from Babylonian captivity and the deliverance of all mankind from sin through the Messiah without mentioning all the history **of the scheme of redemption** that transpires between the two historical events. There is no doubt that the fulfillment of Isaiah's prediction was to be in the Messiah and His gospel (cf. Rom. 10;15.)

(2. <u>v:12 The Lord to return to Zion. **"But you will not leave in haste or go in flight; for the Lord will go before you, the God of Israel will be your rear guard.**</u>

    a. vs. 11-12- Now we come to the practical application of the prophecy of the coming Messenger and His message. How are these people of Isaiah's day or the people of the Babylonian captivity to relate to a prophecy of something that is so far off in the future? On account of the absolute certainty that Jehovah is going to eventually send His Messenger with the good tiding of salvation, and on account of the certainty that Jehovah is going to take the first step toward that end delivering the Jews from "wasted" and "ruined" by pagan oppressors; this news should lift up their spirit and sing of their salvation. This would, of course, take faith because it was not as yet "seen." **(32)**

20. **THE SERVANT TO BE EXALTED -ISAIAH Ch. (52:13-53:12)**

    a. Isaiah *52:13-15,* **The reaction of the nations And the suffering and Glory of the Servant.**

b. **Vs.13-15, "See, my servant will act wisely; he will be raised and lifted up and highly exalted. (14) Just as there were many who were appalled at him, his appearance was disfigured beyond that of any man and his form marred beyond human likeness,(15) So will he sprinkle many nations and kings will shut their mouths because of him. For what they were not told, they will see, and what they have not heard, they will understand."**

(1. **Vs.13-15- SUCCESS OF THE SUFFERING SERVANT. The Hebrew word YASEKKIYL is** the infinitive of SAKAL and may be translated 'to prosper; to have success," instead of "deal wisely." This translation would fit the context. The affirmation of Jehovah is that His Servant shall succeed in fulfilling all the prediction made (through Isaiah) of ultimate deliverance, redemption and glorification of Zion. The Servant Messenger-Messiah of Jehovah will be exalted to the highest degree. Zion has suffered and will suffer much from the days of Isaiah until God comes and establish His reign among men. Verse 15 is in antithesis to verse 14 and emphasizes the contrast between what the Servant first appeared to be and what He later was acknowledged to be. The "thee" (K.J.V.) "him" (N.I.V.) of verse 14 is therefore the Servant-Messiah (Not Israel). Men will be shocked at His humble demeanor. He claimed to be king of the Jews-Messiah, but He did not in any way fulfill human presuppositions as to messianic royalty. The Servant will **sprinkle** people in **many nations.** "Sprinkle" is associated with cleansing by the priest under the Mosaic Law (Lev. 4:6; 8:11; 14:7). This Servant, whom many have not considered important at all, will be seen from a new perspective. Men will be shocked at His humiliation and the nations or Gentiles will be startled at developing

events surrounding His humiliation (The cross) but the death and resurrection will be world wide.

21. ATONE, Isaiah ch. 53.

a. **The report of the death of the Servant (53:1-12).**

b. **V. 1-3.** <u>**"Who has believed our message and to whom has the arm of the Lord been revealed? (2) He grew up before him like a tender shoot, and like a root out of dry ground. He had no beauty or majesty to attract us to him, nothing in his appearance that we should desire him. (3) He was despised and rejected by men, a man of sorrows, and familiar with suffering, Like one from whom men hide their faces he was despised, and we esteemed him not."**</u>

(1. **REJECTED:** Chapter 53 Isaiah is predictive present tense. It is as if the servant has come, been rejected, slaughtered and the people of Israel are looking at it all in retrospect, (as a past event?) The overall reaction of the nation to Jesus' claims to be the Messiah was scoffing, mockery, rejection and persecution. He gained a few disciples, but at the arrest in Gethsemane, they all fled from Him (Mk. 1`4:50).

(2. <u>**Vs. 4-6 Surely he took up our infirmities and carried our sorrows, yet we considered him stricken by God, smitten by him, and afflicted. (5) But he was pierced for our transgressions, he was crushed for our iniquities; the punishment that brought us peace was upon him, and by his wounds we are healed. (6) We all, like sheep, have gone astray, each of us has turned to his own way; and the Lord has laid on him the iniquity of us all."**</u>

(3. Grace:53: Vs. 4-6, Pierced, crushed, punishment and wounds. Unusual pain, sorrow and grief was equated with unusual guilt in the ancient world. The man born blind was marked as a sinner both by the disciples of Jesus and the Pharisees (cf. John 9:1ff). Unusual pain, sorrow and grief were the sign of one's guilt in the ancient world. Job's friends told Him that calamities were punishment from God for his sinfulness (Job3:7-8; 8:4; 11:6 and 15:1-6). And the Jews showed their prejudice against Jesus by mocking Him as a criminal at His crucifixion, and accused Jesus of blasphemy and pointed to His violation of their traditions and His eating with sinners as proof that God was punishing Him. Not realizing that the Servant bore the consequences of their sin. He was taking **our infirmities and sorrows upon Himself**. His obedience to the Father was what counted (cf. Philippians 2:8). His death satisfied the wrath of God against sin and allows Him to "overlook" the sins of the nation (and of others who believed and obey him) because they have been paid for by the Servant's death.(I Cor. 15:3)

(4. 53:7-9, "He was oppressed and afflicted, yet he did not open his mouth; he was led like a lamb to the slaughter, and as a sheep before her shearers is silent, so he did not open his mouth. (8) By oppression and judgment he was taken away. And who can speak of his descendants? For he was cut off from the land of the living; for the transgression of my people he was stricken. (9) He was assigned a grave with the wicked, and with the rich in his death, though he had done no violence, nor was any deceit in his mouth."

c. **GOODNESS OF CHRIST**: God's Servant was innocent and totally submissive. He said nothing to answer the charges of the Sanhedrin (Mt. 26:63). He did not open

His mouth! The great capsulation of the atonement is Romans 3:21-26. The real suffering of the Servant was spiritual, not physical. Many men have suffered physically (perhaps even more torture than crucifixion), but He was innocent, without sin, and actually became sin and suffered spiritual separation (death) from the Father for those who actually deserved it

It is interesting to note that the Hebrew verb MEHOLAL translated WOUNDED means literally PIERCED, PERFORATED, a precise prophecy of the piercing of Christ's body by the Roman soldier (John 19;34-37).

d. <u>Isaiah 53:10-12 "Yet it was the Lord's will to crush him and cause him to suffer, and though the Lord makes his life a guilt offering, he will see his offspring and prolong his days, and the will of the Lord will prosper in his hand. (11) After the suffering of his soul, he will see the light of life and be satisfied; by his knowledge my righteous servant will justify many, and he will bear their iniquities. (12) Therefore I will give him a portion among the great, and he will divide the spoils with the strong, because he poured out his life into death, and was numbered with the transgressors. For he bore the sin of many, and made intercession for the transgressors."</u>

(1. The power is in the resurrection and Christianity not in the esthetic value of great cathedrals, somber ritual and tradition, nor emotionalism but in the historical fact of the resurrection of Christ.

(a. Gives hope that is living (I Pet. 1:3).
(b. Brings joy unspeakable and full of glory (I John 1:1-4).
(c. A man's sin may really be forgiven.
(d. Christ is coming again.
(e. No one will be saved who has not clothed himself with Christ. (Gal. 3:26).

(f. The Bible is God's Word.

(g. The resurrection of Christ makes all the above imperative. There is no middle ground on any of this because His resurrection establishes beyond any question Hisdeity and His authority.

(2. Vs. 10-12- The Servant shall produce "seed" or descendants. He shall have a family, but it will be a spiritual family (cf. Rom. 9:8; Gal. 3:20; 3:23-29). So, it is in being lifted up He will draw men to Him (cf. Jh. 3:14-15; 8:28; 12:32). He shall fall to the ground like a grain of wheat and die, and then bear much fruit (Jh. 12:23-26). And the delight of Jehovah shall succeed through His efforts. The delight of God is, of course, His eternal plan for the redemption of man! Because of His Servant's victory over sin, Satan and death, Jehovah "God" will exalt Him above every other man. The exaltation of the Servant of Jehovah is clearly predicted by the prophet earlier (Isa. 49:7; 52:15).

(3. Vs. 10, The Lord's **WILL, is a Hebrew word KHAPHETZ means "delight" or "desired"** and indicates that the death of the Messiah involved more than an unfeeling, deterministic plan of an unfeeling God. A sinful man could not understand how God could delight in the death of His Son, but He did. **(33)**

22. Salvation to come from the Servant (Isaiah Chap. 54-59)

a. RECONCILED (restore):54:1-8, **"Sing, O barren woman, you who never bore a child; burst into song, shout for joy, you who were never in labor; because more are the children of the desolate woman than of her who has a husband," (2) "Enlarge the place of your tent, stretch your tent curtains wide, do not hold back; lengthen your cords, strengthen your stakes.**

(3) For you will spread out to the right and to the left; your descendants will dispossess nations and settle in their desolate cities." (4)"Do not be afraid; you will not suffer shame. Do not fear disgrace; you will not be humiliated. You will forget the shame of your youth and remember no more the reproach of your widowhood. (5) For your maker is your husband-the Lord Almighty is his name, the Holy One of Israel is your Redeemer; he is called the God of all the earth. (6) The Lord will call you back as if you were a wife deserted and distressed in spirit, a wife who married young, only to be rejected." Says your God. (7)For a brief moment I will abandon you, but with deep compassion I will bring you back. (8) In a surge of anger I hid my face from you for a moment, but with everlasting kindness I will have compassion on you," says the Lord your Redeemer."

(1. Isa. 54 vs. 1-4; INHABIT; The result of the Suffering Servant's redemptive work (Isa. 52:13-53:12) shall be a prolific spiritual offspring. He is to "bring many sons to glory" (Heb. 2:10-13). That is why Zion (God's faithful remnant in the O.T. which will become His church in the N.T. is told to "break forth into singing." The physical descendants of Abraham (cf. Gen. 12:1-3; 17:2-8, **etc.) did not produce spiritually as they** should have.

Most turned to idolatry and sin against God by turning away from His laws. Jerusalem, the "Holy" city, was without spiritual children except for a small remnant of faithful (cf. Isa. 8:16). But when the Servant shall complete His work, Israel shall produce spiritual offspring (cf. Gal.3:29). Jerusalem cannot produce because God, her husband has forsaken her because of her sins, she will be given over to captivity for a short time.

(2. Vs. 5-8-REUNITED- Through the Servant, Jehovah will reclaim His "wife." Jehovah will be reunited, remarried to His people in a new covenant relationship (cf. Isa. 56:6-8; Jer. 31:27-34; Ezk. 37:24-28.) The old covenant will pass away and be remembered no more (cf Jer. 3:15-18). The prophet calls upon Zion to give its attention to the promise of Jehovah that He is going to verify His fidelity in a future covenant, which will be everlasting. The future reconciliation promised in 54:1-8, is predicted on the condition that Zion will enter into a covenant relationship with Servant (Jesus) who is to come. The future covenant will not become obsolete like the old covenant which will pass away and be remembered no more (cf. Jer. 3:15-18; Jer. 31:31-34.). Jehovah will obtain the return of His "wife the church', and will be remarried to His people in a new covenant relationship with Jesus who is to come. (cf. Jer. 56:6-8; Jer. 31:27-34; Ezek. 37:24-28; etc.).

(3. Vs. 9-10 The future reconciliation promised in Isaiah 54:1-8 is, of course, predicted on the condition that Zion will enter into covenant relationship with Jehovah through the Suffering Servant who is to come. The phrase," is taught of Jehovah"(K.J.V.) is quoted by Jesus (Jn.6:45) In Jesus' sermon on The Bread of Life; it is telling of the Messiah to come. Isaiah was predicting that the Incarnation Jesus Christ was "the bread come down out of heaven." The peace mentioned in Ezek. 34:25; 37:26) refer to this promise which God had just made. God will give His people lasting peace (cf. Isa. 9:7; 32:17-18; 54:13; 55:12; 66:12; Jer. 30:10; 33:6, 9; 46:27) in the church.

(4. vs. 11-12: When this "marriage" takes place between God and his new Zion, the bride (the church) will be regaled in beauty. The old Zion, having degraded

itself with idolatry and paganism (Jer. 18;12-17), is about to be taken captive and made a "byword" among the nations. The old Zion will suffer shame, humiliation and mocking. The old Zion will be loathed as a harlot (cf. Ezek. 16;1-52), But Jehovah will restore her fortunes and make her the beautiful, New Zion (Ezek. 16:53-63). Vs. 13-17. **(34)**

23. Salvation for the Gentiles "Invitation to the thirsty" (Isaiah ch. 55)

A. EVIDENCE-1-5.

1. **Vs. 1-5, "Come, all you who are thirsty, come to the water; and you who have no money, come, buy and eat! Come, buy wine and milk without money and without cost. (2) Why spend money on what is not bread, and your labor on what does not satisfy? Listen; listen to me, and eat what is good, and your soul will delight in the richest of fare. (3)"Give ear and come to me; hear me that your soul may live. I will make an ever lasting covenant with you, my faithful love promised to David." (4) "See, I have made him a witness to the people, a leader and commander of the peoples. (5) Surely you will summon nations you know not, and nations that do not know you will hasten to you, because of the Lord your God, the Holy One of Israel, for he has endowed you with splendor."**

   a. 1-2; Isaiah predicted and explained that **Redemption** was through the Suffering Servant. (ch. 53:1-2) The Israelites are excepted to participate in the redemption through their relationship (ch.54). All who realize their need of the substance of life are invited to come and receive freely the saving grace of God. In the N.T. Christ and His apostles portray the blessings of God's grace. Paul's letter to the Romans declares that salvation is by grace (Eph. 2:1-10), but it is faith that gives us access into that grace (Rom. 5:2).

The point of these verses is that God's provision of **redemption** through the Servant shall be by grace. Peter makes it plain that the O.T. prophets predicted salvation by grace (I Pet. 1:10-12). The blessings God gives them are without **cost.** Salvation is a free gift of God, whether it refers to spiritual redemption or physical deliverance. Probably both are intended here.

b. **Vs. 3-5, Faithfulness;** Zion is called to give its attention to the promise of God that he is going to verify his faithfulness in a future covenant relationship which will be everlasting. The future covenant will not become obsolete like the old covenant which will not last (cf. Jer. 3:15-18; Jer. 31:31-34) The future covenant will be eternal; it will be through the covenant of David! (The promise of an eternal king to sit upon David's throne for ever) (cf. II Sam. 7), which the Lord promises that David's line would continue forever. Paul paraphrases Isaiah 55:3 in Acts 13:34, and indicates it was fulfilled in the death and resurrection of Jesus Christ. Chapter 55 is messianic!

c. Genesis 49:10 "The scepter will not depart from Judah, nor the ruler's staff from between his feet until he comes to whom it belongs and the obedience of the nations is his.

24. REPENTANCE to SALVATION Isaiah ch.55:6-7.

1. <u>**Vs. 6-7, "Seek the Lord while he may be found; call on him while he is near. (7) Let the wicked forsake his**</u>

way and the evil man his thoughts. Let him turn to the Lord, and he will have mercy on him, and to our God, for he will freely pardon."

a. V.6-7; REPENTANCE ; The favor (grace) and the faithfulness (verified in the work of the Servant) of Jehovah's promised everlasting covenant is appropriated through repentance in accordance with the revealed word of God. (Eph. 2:8-10) And obeying the word of God. (cf. Acts 2:38).

25. REVELATION; Isaiah ch.55:8-11.

1. **Vs.8-11. "For my thoughts are not your thoughts, neither are your ways my ways," declares the Lord. (9) As the heavens are higher than the earth, so are my ways higher than your ways and my thoughts than your thoughts. (10) As the rain and the snow come down from heaven, and do not return to it without watering the earth and making it bud and flourish, so that it yields seed for the sower and bread for the eater, (11) so is my word that goes out from my mouth: It will not return to me empty, but will accomplish what I desire and achieve the purpose for which I sent it.**

    a. The salvation plan of God for the **redemption** of the world goes beyond mans thinking or experience. Grace will not make sense in the world. Therefore, man refuses to accept God's plan because God's plan is beyond man's wisdom. (Isaiah 55:11-13-) **"You will go out in joy and be led forth in peace; the mountains and hills will burst into song before you, and all the trees of the field will clap their hands. Instead of the thorn bush will grow the pine tree, and, and instead of briers the myrtle will grow . . ."** The whole creation is rejoicing at Zion's redemption. These verses are a figurative description of the rejoicing the whole creation is going to enter in through the work of the Servant. (cf. Rom. 8:18-25) **(35)**

(1). God does change people and their lives.

26. Gentiles included in Israel's blessings and accusation against the wicked. (Isaiah ch. 56)

1. **Salvation for others (56:1-8)**

2. **"56. 1-2 "This is what the Lord says: "Maintain justice and do what is right, for my salvation is close at hand and my righteousness will soon be revealed. (2) Blessed is the man who does this, the man who holds it fast, who keeps the Sabbath without desecrating it and keeps his hand from doing any evil."**

   a. Vs. 1-2 New Covenant revealed; **Jeremiah 31:31-33; "... I will make a new covenant .... 33; "I will put my law in their minds and write it on their hearts."** On the basis of the Suffering Servant's atonement and the offer of a new covenant relationship through His accomplishment, the emphasis is now put on man's espousal or choice of the covenant. Jehovah's salvation is "near"! In His salvation, His righteousness will be revealed (cf. Rom. 1:17; 3:21-26). **Do what is right** (cf. 1:17) because God's **salvation** (spiritual deliverance and physical protection) will come soon. Again Isaiah linked present behavior with future salvation and blessings.

3. **Vss.3-8 "Let no foreigner who has bound himself to the Lord say, "The Lord will surely exclude me from his people." And let not any eunuch complain, "I am only a dry tree." (4) For this is what the Lord says: "To the eunuchs, who keep my Sabbaths, who choose**

what pleases me and hold fast to my covenant- (5) to them I will give within my temple and its walls a memorial and a name better than my sons and daughters; I will give them an everlasting name that will not be cut off. (6) And foreigners who bind themselves to the Lord to serve him, to love the name of the Lord, and to worship him, all who keep the Sabbath without desecration and who hold fast to my covenant (7) these I will bring to my holy mountain and give them joy in my house of prayer. Their burnt offerings and sacrifices will be accepted on my altar; for my house will be called a house of prayer for all nations." (8) The Sovereign Lord declares, he who gathers the exiles of Israel; "I will gather still others to them besides those already gathered."

a. **Vs.3-8, Foreigners** vs.3, (Heb. Word -**nakerily,**) and sojourners (Heb. **ger.**) might become citizens and members of the covenant people but they were prohibited from participating in full fellowship with people of the land (cf. Ex. 12:43-49; Lev. 16:29; 17:12; 18:26.) etc.

Eunuchs were also barred from the temple of God (Der. 23:1). Naturally, when they heard Isaiah's predictions that in the messianic age to come they would become a citizen, and have fellowship with the people and not be outcast you can know their joy. Jehovah will bring them and (Gentles) to Zion (Heb. 12:22ff.), the N.T. church (cf. Isa. 2:1-4). All will be restored to loving fellowship with the Messiah and His new covenant. The Messiah's sacrifice (once for all, cf. Heb. 10:1-18) will atone for all men's sins. God's new house, Zion, will be for men of all nations (Eph. 1:11-22) a house of prayer (cf. Mk. 11:17). **(36)**

27. **Condemnation for the wicked, and God's accusation against them. (Isaiah 56:9; 57:2-1.**

1. **Ch. 57:1-2 THE RIGHTEOUS:**

2. **Ch. 57:14-21 The Lord's promise of forgiveness.**

3. v.16-21- RECONCILIATION, Although the Lord has recounted the sorceries, sensualities and stupidities of Israel and although He has smitten them in the past (and will smite them again in captivity), He now addresses Himself to the future reconciliation. He is going to accomplish through the Servant which will begin in the restoration from the captivity and be offered to all mankind through covenant relationship.

28. **THE RESTORATION TO COME BY GOD, (Isaiah 58-60)**

1. *Obedience required and Wholeness to the wise who keeps no covenant with the Lord (ch. 58)*

2. **Salvation to come by God and wrath of the Lord (Isaiah 59).**

3. **REWARD OF ZION and WEALTH OF THE NATIONS-Isaiah 60.**

29. **THE COMING OF THE MESSIAH AND THE COMING OF THE FATHER (ISAIAH 61:1-63:6)**

1. The coming of the Messiah, rejoicing of Zion (Isaiah 61)

   a. Isaiah 61:1-7 "The spirit of the Sovereign Lord is on me, because the Lord has anointed me to preach good news to the poor. He has sent me to bind up the brokenhearted, to proclaim freedom for the captives and to release from darkness for the prisoners, (2) to proclaim the year of the Lord's favor and the day of vengeance of our God, to comfort all who mourn, (3) and provide for those who grieve in Zion, to bestow on them a crown of beauty instead of ashes, the oil of gladness instead of mourning, and a garment of praise instead of a spirit of despair. They will be called oaks of righteousness, a planting of the Lord for the display of his splendor." (4) They will rebuild the ancient ruins and restore the places long devastated; they will renew the ruined cities that have been devastated for generations." (5) Aliens will shepherd your flocks; foreigners will work your fields and vineyards. (6) And you will be called priests of the Lord, you will be named ministers of our God. You will feed on the wealth of nations, and in their riches you will boast." (7) Instead of their shame my people will receive a double portion, and instead of disgrace they will rejoice in their inheritance; and so they will inherit a double portion in their land, and everlasting joy will be theirs."

(1. Vs.1-2, MESSSAGE; The "me" of verse one can be none other than the Servant of Jehovah, the Messiah. Jesus himself, who read this in the synagogue (it was perhaps the reading for that day says, "The Spirit of the Lord is on me, because he has anointed me to preach good news to the poor. He has sent me to proclaim freedom for the prisoners and recovery of sight for the blind, to release the oppressed, to proclaim the year of the Lord's" Luke 4:21 Jesus says, "Today this scripture is fulfilled in your hearing." We have the divine word that the Servant Himself was to preach the good news of salvation to the world.

(2. Vs. 3-4, MISSION: The Hebrew word **PHE'ER,** translated **GARLAND,** means more precisely, an ornamental headdress, or adorning tiara. The Servant-Messiah accomplishes more than conquest, He brings coronation to His people (cf. Rom. 8:31-39). He makes it possible for believers to "sit with Him in the heavenly places" (Eph. 2:6). His followers are crowned and reign with Him over death and all other circumstances. (cf. I Cor. 5:9-1; Heb. 11:7; I Cor. 3:21-22; Rev. 5:10).

(3. Vs. 5-6, JOINING: The Hebrew word "**zarim**" is translated "strangers" AND MEANS, "LOATHED-ONE, BARBARIANS, ENEMIES, EXCLUDED-ONES, BEN-NEKAR is Hebrew for SONS OF THE ALIEN OR SONS OF THE FOREIGNER. When the Messiah-Servant came crying (shouting) aloud the time of the messianic Jubilee (the time of the Lord's pleasure), those who had been excluded, alienated from covenant relationship to Jehovah were to be given an invitation to join the chosen people in serving and ministering to him. Jesus in the synagogue at Nazareth apparently closed the scroll of Isaiah before He read beyond verses 1-2 of this chapter. He did not read the verses now under consideration, but He implied them in His reference to the mercy shown by Jehovah to the Gentiles (Lk. 4;23-27) Paul' statement to the Gentiles in Eph. 2:11-22 is certainly the fulfillment of this. Isaiah is predicting that the nations (**GOIYM**) (Gentiles) will be included in the messianic age as God's people (Isa. 2;1-4; 19;23-25; 25;6-12; etc. The Jewish Apocrypha (non-canonical writing) however, reflect the humanistic, materialistic interpretation of such prophecies as those of Isaiah here concerning God's purposes for the Gentiles in the messianic age. These apocryphal

writings show a liberal attitude of the Jewish
mind toward the Gentiles during a time of relative
freedom and peace for the Jews in the days of
the Maccabeans, but an intensifying bitterness
and hatred for the Gentiles as the oppression of
Rome increased until the days of Jesus and the
hotheaded Zealots and Sicarii eventually stirred
up the rebellion and insurrection that brought
about the destruction of Jerusalem and the Jewish
nation in A.D. 70. According to I Enoch 10:21,
(WRITTEN ABOUT 164 B.C., all the Gentiles
will become righteous and offer to God their
adoration and worship. In the Sibylline Oracles
III (written about 150 B.C.); from every land the
Gentiles will make their way in the procession of
God, bringing frankincense and gifts to the house
of God, and in the coming messianic kingdom
they have a share in the blessings that it brings.
What God meant in Isaiah 61 was, of course,
just the opposite of the common Jewish concept.
Many of the Jews learned this with great difficulty
but rejoiced once it became apparent that it was
the will of God. (cf Acts 9:1-16; 10:34-43; 11:18;
13:44-52; 15:12-21; Gal. 2:11ff., etc.

b. **Isaiah 61:8-11, "For I, the Lord, love justice; I
    hate robbery and iniquity. In my faithfulness I will
    reward them and make an everlasting covenant
    with them. (9) Their descendants will be known
    among the nations and their offspring among the
    peoples. All who see them will acknowledge that
    they are a people the Lord has blessed. (10) I delight
    greatly in the Lord; my soul rejoices in my God.
    For he has clothed me with garments of salvation
    and arrayed me in a robe of righteousness, as a
    bridegroom adorns his head like a priest, and as
    a bride adorns herself with her jewels. (11) For as
    the soil makes the sprout come up and a garden**

causes seeds to grow, so the Sovereign Lord will make righteousness and praise spring up before all nations."

(4. RENOWN: Vs. 8-9, Zion will one day rejoice because she shall be made famous. The reason she shall be made famous, however, will not be due to her own merit but because God is who He is . . .

The loyalty Jehovah will reward, will be that of the sinless Servant; but the Servant will impute His perfect meritorious (honor) obedience (Heb. 10:5-10) to all who by faith and covenant keeping become citizens of the new Zion . . . . The "seed" and "offspring" of New Zion will be renowned among the Gentiles. The people of the Messiah (Christians) were known throughout the Roman world of the first century (and ever after) for their faith, obedience and love (cf. Acts 2:47; 4:13, 33: Rom. 16:19: I Thiss. 1:8-10: Phil. 4-7; I Peter 4:4) . . . The goodness and blessedness and joy of the lives of citizens of Zion will be acknowledged by the whole world. The Messiah's people are ("blessed with every spiritual blessing in the heavenly places" Eph. 1:3)

(5. **Vs. 10**-New Zion is rejoicing in the Lord because the Lord has clothed her in salvation and righteousness. The church is all dressed up like someone waiting for a wedding! (cf. Eph. 5:25-27; Rev. 19:6-10).

(1. Gal. 3:26-29, "you are all sons of God through faith in Christ Jesus (27 for all of you who were baptized into Christ have clothed yourselves with Christ. (28) There is neither Jew nor Greek, slave nor free, male nor

female, for you are all one in Christ Jesus.
(29) If you belong to Christ, then you are
Abraham's seed, and heirs according to the
promise.

(6. <u>Vs. 11</u>- Isaiah affirms the faithfulness of Jehovah
to keep his word. God's word always produces it,
and always comes to pass. (Isa. 55:10-11). **(37)**

30. PREPARATION FOR the COMING of the LORD (Isaiah 62)

1. **Zion new name Ch. 62:1-5.**

2. **Vs.1-3**: Jehovah dare not remain "**Khashah**" (silent) or
"**shakat**" (inactive) any longer in relationship to Zion.
Jehovah will not rest again until He has made Zion so
righteous her splendor and glory will be as blindingly
evident as the sun in the heavens or a lamp shining in
pitch darkness. What God is going to do in glorifying
Zion, the whole world shall see. Everything about Zion
will be new; it will not be by the law keeping, but by
grace are you saved. (Eph. 2:8-9). This new Zion was
predicted by other prophets (Jer. 3:15-17; 33:16; Ezk.
48:35). This prophecy was fulfilled when God's New
Covenant people began to be called "Christians" (cf.
Acts 11:26).

3. Vs. 4-5. The point of the name change appears to be
focused on the changed relationship of God toward His
people. He will no longer call them "**ezuvah**" (forsaken)
or "**shemamah**" (desolate). God will eventually call
His people "**khephzi-bah**" (My Delight is in Her)
and "**ezuah**" (Married). The emphasis on marriage
is descriptive of the new relationship and given a new
name.

(1. **Note-Matt. 25:1-13.**

(2. **Acts 11:26, Called Christians.**

31. **Protection and New Nourishment 62:6-9.**

    a. **PROTECTION**: Vs.6-7,

    b. **PROVISION:, Vs.8-9.**

    c. Isaiah 62:**10-12, SEPARATED**: The admonition to Judah here is that she must prepare to separate herself from paganism in order that she may become the remnant through which Jehovah will build New Zion (the redeemed messianic church). Judah will soon go into captivity. There she will be surrounded by the idolatry and carnality with which she is so enamored in her own land. It will be a great temptation to all the Jews to compromise the truth of God's revelation and take up with paganism to the extent that when the time comes to return to Palestine and restore the Jewish commonwealth they will all decide to remain in Babylon . . . . Now the Lord is calling her back to her divine mission and prediction that there will be a remnant who will choose to fulfill this mission and eventually form New Zion (the church) which will draw people from all nations to her. Jehovah will accomplish Zion's redemption, He will pay the price (in the Messiah). But Zion must exercise her will and accept that salvation by faith, requires an obedience to the covenant terms. Repentance and faith requires an obedient turning away from sin, separating oneself deliberately and willingly from all that God prohibits and living deliberately and willingly what God commands. Covenant terms for New Zion involves obedience in baptism (immersion in water), Acts 2:38; 8 :12-13; 8:38-39; 10:47; 16:15 Rom. 6:1-6; Gal. 3:26-27; I Pet.3:21.

    d. **Vs. 12, SANCTIFIED:** When Zion separates itself from paganism and accepts the Lord's salvation, she shall be acknowledged and (Holy).

32. Restlessness of Zion, Chap, 63-64.

1. Predicted vendication-63:1-9

    a. Conquest-vs.1-6.
    b. Celebration-vs. 7-9

2. Prayer for victory-63:10-14.

    a. Resisting His Spirit-vs.10.
    b. Remembering His Spirit-vs. 11-13.
    c. The 10 commandments (Good) Psa. 51:11; 142:10. etc.(Better) Incarnate Son-John. 14:17.etc. (Best) Glorified Christ John. 16:7; Acts. 2:33.
    d. Resting In His Spirit-14.

3. Petition of victims-63:15-19.

    a. Disowned-vs. 15-17
    b. Dispossessed-vs.18-19.

33. Restlessness of Zion continued from Chap. 63-64.

1. Penitently vexed (disturbed)—64:1-7.

    a. Cry-vs. 1-3.
    b. Confession-vs. 4-7.

2. Plea for verification-64:8-12.

34. Refining of Zion with Judgment and Salvation Isaiah ch. 65.

1. Refining of Zion-(cleansed) vs. 1-12.
2. Ch. 65:1-7.Sin Repaid: It may have appeared up to this point in Isaiah's prophesy that he was pronouncing doom upon the whole nation. However, the prayer in chapter

64 shows that there was a small remnant of people who had turned to the Lord for help . . . .

Those who blaspheme the Lord will be recompensed with judgment; those who trust Him will become a "seed" and provide heirs to Judah's promised.

3. **Seed Replanted; 65:8-12- "This is what the Lord says; "As when juice is still in a cluster of grapes and men say, "Don't destroy it, there is yet some good in it, so will I do in behalf of my servant; I will not destroy them all. I will bring forth descendants from Jacob, and from Judah those who will possess my mountains; my chosen people will inherit them, and there will my servants live. (10) Sharon will become a pasture for flocks and the Valley of Achor a resting-place for herds, for my people who seek me. (11) But as for you who forsake the Lord and forget my holy mountain, who spread a table for Fortune and will bowls of mixed wine for Destiny, (12) I will destine you for the sword, and you will all bend down for the slaughter; for I called but you did not answer, I spoke but you did not listen. You did evil in my sight and chose what displeases me."**

   a. **Ch.65.Vs. 8-12,** Out of the captivities God will refine a small remnant. When a keeper (husbandman) of a vineyard gathers clusters of grapes he does not throw away a whole cluster if he sees some good grapes in it. So Jehovah saw in this rotten nation a few good people who would be a blessing to the world and form the messianic remnant. The Lord did not destroy the whole nation, (cf. Jer. 46:28). One is much more impressed with the promise of God to Isaiah concerning the 'holy seed' (cf. Isa. 6:13). God is going to bring forth a **"seed out of Jacob** (Isa. 56:9) and this seed shall be replanted in the land and it shall "produce servants" to inherit the spiritual blessings which shall come through the messianic kingdom. Those who came to Zion, the N/T. church, inherited Jehovah's mountain (cf. Heb. 12:22-29). Jehovah promised to multiply the "seed" to inherit the messianic promises (cf. II Sam. 7:12-17; Isa. 44:3; 54:3; 59:21; 66:22; Jer. 33:19-22).

b. **NURTURED; <u>Ch.65 ;13-16.</u> "Therefore this is what the Sovereign Lord says: "My servants will eat, but you will go hungry; my servants will drink, but you will go thirsty; my servants will rejoice, but you will be put to shame. (14) My servants will sing out of the joy of their hearts, but you will cry out from anguish of heart and wail in brokenness of spirit.**

(15) You will leave your name to my chosen ones as a curse; the Sovereign Lord will put you to death, but to his servants he will give another name. (16) Whoever invokes a blessing in the land will do so by the God of truth; he who takes on oath in the land will swear by the God of truth. For the past troubles will be forgotten and hidden from my eyes."

c. **VS.13-14-NURTURED**; Continuing the idea of a refined Zion and the contrast between the "good grapes and the bad grapes" the Lord is now talking about the difference in the refining process. Even those who were not called by His name, who do find Him and call upon Him and become obedient servants, He will fill with spiritual nutrition growth and satisfaction. Of course, Isaiah is writing of future spiritual things in physical terminology. The New covenant scriptures make it plain that God's richest blessings are spiritual (cf. Eph. 1:3) Those who hunger and thirst after righteousness will be filled (Mt. 5:6); who seek the Bread of Life shall have it

(Jn. 6:52-65); those who thirst for the Water of Life shall drink of it (Jn. 4:13; 7:37-39.

d. **Vs. 15-16. NAMED**: These verses (Isa. 65:15-16) clearly show that the genetic nation of Israel is not synonymous with God's chosen (cf. also Rom. 2:28-29). In the light of this precise statement that God is going to slay the disobedient nation and call his servants by another name, what scriptural reason is there for expecting a future resurrection of genetic Israel? Ezekiel 37 undoubtedly refers to the restoration of Judah after the Babylonian captivity in 536 B.C. Certainly the nation that was restored then cannot be fulfillment of Isaiah 65:13-16; neither can the present-day Israel!

e. **NEW NAME:** What God is going to do in glorifying Zion, the whole world shall see. And it shall be totally different from what Zion has been before; she shall have to be called by a new name. Everything about her will be new; old terminology will be inadequate. This wholly new Zion is predicted by other prophets (Jer. 3:15-17; 33:16; Ezk. 48:35) This prophecy was fulfilled when God's New Covenant people began to be called "Christians: (Cf. Acts 11:26). It is fitting that those "married" to Christ should be called "Christians" (cf. Jn. 3:31-36; Eph. 5:21-33; Rev. 19:6-8; 21:2; 22:17**.**) (38)

4. **Isaiah 65:17-25; NEW HEAVEN and a NEW EARTH- "Behold, I will create a new heaven and a new earth. The former things will not be remembered, nor will they come to mind. (18) But be glad and rejoice forever in what I will create. (19) I will rejoice over Jerusalem and take delight in my people; the sound of weeping and of crying will be heard in it no more. (20) Never again will there be in it an infant who lives but a few days, or an old man who does not live out**

his years; he who dies at a hundred will be thought a mere youth; he who fails to reach a hundred will be considered accursed. (21) They will build houses and dwell in them; they will plant vineyards and eat their fruit". (22) No longer will they build houses and others live in them, or plant and others eat. For as the days of a tree, so will be the days of my people; my chosen ones will long enjoy the works of their hands. (23) They will not toil in vain or bear children doomed to misfortune; for they will be a people blessed by the Lord, they and their descendants with them. (24) Before they call I will answer; while they are still speaking I will hear. (25) The wolf and the lamb will feed together, and the lion will eat straw like the ox, but dust will be the serpent's food. They will neither harm nor destroy on all my holy mountain," says the Lord".

a. Is this a prediction of the end of time? If so, why speak of longevity of life in verse 20?

b. Does verse 25 mean same as Isaiah 11:6-9? (Yes). I suggest that you check it out for yourself!

c. **Ch.65, Vs. 17-19, PERSONALITY**: In verse 16 Isaiah promised new Zion, "the former troubles are forgotten." Now the prophet shows why the former troubles will be forgotten; Jehovah is going to create an entirely new order. The Hebrew verb BARA is translated CREATE and is used in the Hebrew GAL stem only with God as the subject. "New Jerusalem, the new covenant, and the old will not be remembered (cf. Jer. 3:15-17; 31:31-34). In Hebrews 2:5-9 we are told that Christ came to restore man to the dominion over "the world to come" which man lost when he sinned in the garden of Eden. What God has done by Christ's redemptive work and establishment of the church, is therefore, the new creation. Hebrews 12:27

indicates that the "old order" (Judaism, or Mosaic covenant) was "shaken" (destroyed) in order that what cannot be shaken may remain. Paul indicates that "the new covenant relationship" is the "new creation." (cf. II Cor. 5:16-21; Gal. 6:15-16.)

d. **Ch.65, Vs. 20, IMMORTALITY**: This verse is portraying in figurative language the "immortality" of the citizens of new Zion. It is not as clear as the statement in Isa.25:8, but nevertheless, in context, is teaching the concept of immortality. As we have it in our paraphrase, "There will be no more limited life in My New Jerusalem-neither among the very young nor the very old. Every citizen of new Zion will live in eternal joy.

e. **Ch.65, Vs. 21-25, PROSPERITY:** Everything the citizen of new Zion does, as he conforms to the image of Christ, will produce fruit to Jehovah's glory and satisfaction to the heart of the doer (cf. Cor. 15:58; Rom. 8:28; II Cor. 9:8; Eph. 3:20.) Nothing hurtful will be permitted in New Zion. In God's "holy mountain" (Zion Cf. Heb. 12:22), the place where He dwells, there will be peace and joy.

35. CONCLUSION-Judgement and hope, Isaiah ch. 66.

1. Burial of old Zion, 66:1-6.
2. Birth of new Zion, 66:7-15.
3. Building of Zion, 66:15-24.

   a. The breaking off of the Old and the establishment of the New are coincidental; they are to occur at the same time, within a generation (cf. Mt. 24:34), of the apostles (Peter, James, John, etc.). When the Suffering Servant had made atonement for sin and was raised from the dead destroying the ultimate power of the devil, Israel was to turn to Jehovah and accept citizenship in New Zion (the church). Some did, but a majority did not. Jehovah, in his longsuffering allowed the Jewish nation to retain its city and temple for another 40 years (until 70 A.D.). Christians witnessed the destruction of Jerusalem in 70 A.D. and were reminded of the fate of all who disobey God and reject His Son and warned that a similar fate awaits an unbelieving world when Jesus comes back to earth at the end of time (Mt. 24:51).... Essentially Isaiah's message is that God's great plan to redeem the world involves the incarnation of the Word in the person of the Suffering Servant. The atonement for sin by the Servant; the incorporation into that covenant relationship and formation of a New Zion from all in the world who will believe and accept its terms. **(ISAHAH Volume III by Paul T. Butler, College Press, Joplin, Missouri, copyright, 1978, p.P.7-484.**

   (39)

CHAPTER 11

EZEKIEL

EZEKIEL, God's Spokesmen in a Foreign Land.

A. INTRODUCTION:

1. There are four Old Testament prophets called "major prophets"

   a. Isaiah who prophesied to Judah in the 8Th. Century B.C., around 593-587 B.C.
   b. Jeremiah who prophesied to Judah during the time that Judah was being taken into captivity.
   c. Ezekiel who prophesied to the Jews in Babylon.
   d. Daniel who was among the first captives and prophesied from the King's court in Babylon.
   e. Jeremiah, Ezekiel, and Daniel were all contemporaries; Isaiah was about one hundred years earlier,

B. The Message of Ezekiel: The fall of Jerusalem, and captivity was a necessary measure for God if He was to correct His disobedient people and draw them back from complete and permanent apostasy. It was Ezekiel's prophetic duty to explain that Judah**'s sinful ways** must come to an end. But that would not be the end of the story. God would one day gather His repentant remnant of people back to their home, where they would share in glorious latter-day theocracy. Thus the basic message of Ezekiel is that God is faithful to His eternal purpose. Ezekiel has been called the "father of Judaism" because of the influence he has with Judah ... **Ezekiel's doctrine of the Messiah,** the Messiah is not as prominent in Jeremiah and Ezekiel as in Isaiah. Nevertheless, there is some striking teaching about the promise in this book. The Messiah is represented as a "tender twig" taken from the highest branch of the cedar of Judah's royalty, planted upon a high mountain (Ezek. 17:22-24). He is the one to whom the diadem of Israel's sovereignty rightfully belonged and to whom it would be given after it had been removed from the end of the wicked Zedekiah (Ezek. 21:27). The Messianic David will be faithful prince among God's restored people. He will perform all the functions of a true and faithful Shepherd (Ezek. 34:23, 24), ruling over them as king (37:24). This Prince will eat and drink before the Lord in His capacity of special representative of God's people (Ezek. 44:3). **(40)**

EZEKIEL by James E. Smith; College Press, Joplin, Missouri. (Copyright 1979, Third Printing, 1989.

C. **THE KING; A LOWLY VINE, EZEK. Ch. 17:1-21.**

1. **Chapter 17 Ezekiel turns his attention to King Zedekiah back in Jerusalem. This vassal king had committed an act of treachery against Nebuchadnezzar by breaking his solemn oath of allegiance to Babylon in seeking military aid from Egypt. In this oracle delivered shortly before 586 B.C. Ezekiel predicts the extinction of Zedekiah's dynasty and the fall of Jerusalem.**

D. **MESSIAH; THE STATELY CEDAR 17:22-24.**

1. **Ezekiel Ch. 17:22-24 <u>"This is what the Sovereign Lord says: I myself will take a shoot from the top of a</u>**

cedar and plant it; I will brak off a tender sprig from its topmost shoots and plant it on a high and lofty mountain. (23) On the mountain heights of Israel I will plant it; it will produce branches and bear fruit and become a splendid cedar. Birds of every kind will nest in it; they will find shelter in the shade of its branches. (24) All the trees of the field will know that I the Lord bring down the tall tree and make the low tree grow tall. I dry up the green tree and make the dry tree flourish. "I the Lord have spoken, and I will do it."

a. The message of doom in the preceding parable and application is tempered by a word of hope in verses 22-24. God in His sovereign grace is about to act. Nebuchadnezzer had cut a twig from that same cedar and had removed it from Babylon and planted it in a city of traders (cf. vv. 3f). But God would now cut a twig from that some royal cedar tree and plant it upon a high mountain (v.22). The basic idea is that the Davidic dynasty would be reinstated and would achieve a prominence, which it had not heretofore enjoyed. The Messiah King of the house of David is in view here. Jesus of Nazareth now occupies the throne of David and rules over the New Israel of God. The Messianic twig would be prominent, planted in the high mountain of Israel. The cedar-Messianic Jerusalem, the church of Christ—would be stately, i.e., dignified. It would bear fruit. The Messiah heads a royal family of kings and priests (cf. I Pet. 2:9).

Many birds (different nations) would place themselves under the protection of this Messianic Monarch (v. 23). The **(high trees- proud kingdoms-of Ezekiel's days would be cut down or dry up).** The **(low tree- God's people—would be exalted under the leadership of the Messiah.** All people would then realize that it is by the will of God that the haughty are humbled and debased exalted (v.24). **(39)**

E. EZEKIEL'S DOCTRINE OF MAN. Ezek. Ch. 18.

1. Two important doctrines are discussed in chapter 18. In verses 1-20 Ezekiel develops at length the doctrine of individual responsibility and in verse 21-29 he implicitly affirms the doctrine of freedom of the will or self-determination.
2. The Principle of personal Responsibility Ch. 18:1-20.

3. The Potential of personal Repentance Ch. 18:21-32.

F. REPLACEMENT OF CORRUPT LEADERS ; Ezek. 34:11-31.)

1. THE DIVINE SHEPHERD-Ch. 34, 11-22.

a. The good Shepherd-vs. 11-22 "For this is what the Sovereign Lord says: "I myself will search for my sheep and look after them. (12) As a shepherd looks after his scattered flock when he is with them, so will I look after my sheep. I will rescue them from all the places where they were scattered on a day of clouds and darkness. (13) I will bring them out from the nations and gather them from the countries, and I will bring them into their own land. I will pasture them on the mountains of Israel, in the revines and in all the settlements in the land. (14) I will tend them in a good pasture, and the mountain heights of Israel will be their grazing land. There they will lie down in good grazing land, and there they will feed in a rich pasture on the mountains of Israel. (15) I myself will tend my sheep and have them lie down, declares the Sovereign Lord.

(16) I will search for the lost and bring back the strays. I will bind up the injured and strengthen the weak, but the sleek and the strong I will destroy. I will shepherd the flock with justice. (17) As for you, my flock, this is what the Sovereign Lord says: "I will judge between one sheep and another, and between rams and goats.

(18) Is it not enough for you to feed on the good pasture? Must you also trample the rest of your pasture with feet? Is it not enough for you to drink clear water? Must you also muddy the rest with your feet? (19) Must my flock feed on what you have trampled and drink what you have muddied with your feet? (20) Therefore this is what the Sovereign Lord says to them; "See I myself will judge between the fat sheep and the lean sheep. (21) Because you shove with flank and shoulder, butting all the weak sheep with your horns until you have driven them away, (22) I will save my flock, and they will no longer be plundered. I will judge between one sheep and another."

(1. God's people would not be left without a shepherd. The hirelings have been removed from office, the Good Shepherd Himself would take over direct responsibility. He would begin His task by searching out His sheep. His sheep are those who hear and respond to His word (Jh. 10:27. The Good Shepherd **"knows His sheep and His sheep know Him."** (cf. John 10:14)

(2. **v. 11).** The Lord God takes the initiative in reclaiming His own. Wherever they have been scattered the Faithful Shepherd would find them.

(3. **(v. 12).** Then come restoration to Canaan, the Promised Land. There God would feed His flock **(upon the mountains and by the streams.)**

(4. **(vs. 13).** Lush pasture and a secure fold awaited the flock of God in Canaan.

(5. **(v. 14).** The flock, hurt and driven by beasts of pray (unholy nations), would lie down under the watchful care of the Good Shepherd.

(6. (vs. **15-16).** Not like the shepherds of Israel, the Good shepherd would devote special attention to the weak and lost sheep of His flock. He will protect and feed them, as He brings them back to the fold.

(7. **Cf.** Luke 15:3-6 ". . . Rejoice with me, I have found my lost sheep."

(8. (v.17) God would (judge) between members of the flock, between the oppressed poor and their oppressors (Pharisees and Sadducees the Jewish leaders). The latter are referred to here as **(the rams and the goats,)**

2. **The Future Shepherd Ch.34:23-31.**

a. **V. 23-31: "I will place over them one shepherd, my servant David, and he will tend them; he will tend them and be their shepherd, (24) I the Lord will be their God, and my servant David will be prince among them. I the Lord have spoken. (25) I will make a covenant of peace with them and rid the land of wild beasts so that they may live in the desert and sleep in the forest in safety. (26) I will bless them and the places surrounding my hill. I will send down showers in season; there will**

be showers of blessing. (27) The trees of the field will yield their fruit and the ground will yield its crops; the people will be secure in their land. They will know that I am the Lord, when I break the bars of their yoke and rescue them from hands of those who enslaved them (28) They will no longer be plundered by the nations, nor will wild animals devour them. They will live in safety, and no one will make them afraid. (29) I will provide for them a land renowned for its crops, and they will no longer be victims of famine in the land or bear the scorn of the nations.

(30) Then they will know that I, the Lord their God, am with them and that they, the house of Israel, are my people, declares the Sovereign Lord. (31) You my sheep, the sheep of my pasture, are people, and I am your God, declares the Sovereign Lord."

(1. **After** the return from exile and the period of direct divine supervision of the flock, God would set up a shepherd over His people. This Shepherd must be the long-awaited Messiah, a ruler of the house of David. The Davidic dynasty would be restored. The responsibility of feeding and tending the flock of God would be committed to Him (v23). Yahweh would still be their God: but His servant David would be **prince** among them (v.24) What a marvelous **foregleam (or seeing the future)** of the New Testament doctrine of the Father and the Son (vs.24). A new covenant is a prominent feature of the Messianic age (cf. Jer. 31:31). Here it is called a covenant of peace. **(41)**

Ezekiel by James E. Smith; cp. 1979; (College Press, Joplin, Missouri.)

CHAPTER 12

MINOR PROPHETS

MINOR PROPHETS: (By Clinton R. Gill, College Press, Joplin, Missouri, Copyright 1971-1988.

A. MICAH:

1. **Whatever God may have done** in the eons (consecrated) of time touched so briefly in the first eleven chapters of Genesis, it was the call of Abram in Genesis 12:1-3 which set in motion the **"Scheme of Redemption"** that was to climax at Calvary. In the making of the everlasting covenant, established at this call, God revealed to man the only way back to God, by virtue of His unmerited favor made effective through **obedient faith**. The theme of the Bible is the history of this covenant people. It is the record of God's working in the history of His people to **"reconcile the world unto Himself,"** (II Cor. 5:19). The Covenant of Promise first began to be fulfilled in "all that Jesus began to do and to teach (Acts. 1:1) and continues through the new covenant people, the church (Gal. 3:29). Jesus indicated that two things stand written in the Old Testament Scriptures:

(1). that the Christ should suffer and be raised the third day and, **(2)** That repentance and remission of sins should be preached in His name among all the nations beginning at Jerusalem. (Luke 24:44-48). The church thus becomes under the New Covenant the continuing presence of Christ in the world" . . . His body, the fullness of Him that fills all in all . . . "Ephesians. 1:23). JEREMIAH, 23:3, sets down the promise of God to "gather the remnant of my flock out of all countries whither I have driven them." This promise is accompanied by another; (v.5) "The days are coming declares the Lord, when I will raise to David a righteous Branch, a King who will reign wisely and do what is just and right in the land." **(42) ps. 10-11.**

2. The covenant was proposed by God, not man. Man can only respond on God's terms. (Eph. 3:16) The heart of the covenant was the promise that through it all the nations of the earth will be blessed in the seed of Abraham. The New Testament identifies that "seed" as Christ, (Gal. 3:16) And as those baptized into Him (Gal. 3:27-29

    a. **FUTURE EXALTATION and MESSIANIC HOPE-in MICAH,** Sees Jehovah as the Master of all nations. In his prophecy, as well as that of other Old Testament writers may be traced the outline of the way by which God's rule over all men is to be brought about.

    b. People from all nations are to willingly answer the call when He who is Abraham's Seed is born in "Bethlehem. (Micah 5:2-5.) In Micah 2:12,4:7, 5:8, and 7:18, the prophet focuses attention on those few in the nation who were true to the covenant.

    c. **Ch. 2:6. "Do not prophesy," their prophets say. "Do not prophesy about these things: disgrace will not overtake us."** Do not prophesy vs. 6, these are the words of the false prophets and their followers in response to the warning pronounced by prophets of Jehovah. Others than Micah had been rebuked in this same way, (cf. Amos 7:16). Israel was called into being in the beginning because it was God's purpose through them to bless all nations. To do this there must be a once-for-all demonstration that His relationship to His people does not depend upon their racial origin and national identity, but upon their obedient faith.

3. **Micah 2:12-13- Deliverance promised. "I will surely gather all of you, O Jacob; I will surely bring together the remnant of Israel. I will bring them together like sheep in a pen, like a flock in its pasture; the place will throng with people. (13) One who beaks open the way will go up before them; they will break through the gate and go out. Their king will pass through before them, the Lord at their head,"**

   a. The Messianic overtones expressed in the figure of the Lord passing as king before the remnant is obvious. It was David particularly that the Messianic prophecies of the Lord's kinship found their personification. From David's reign on, the Messiah was expected to sit upon "the throne of His Father David. **"When your days are over and you go to be with your father, I will raise up your offspring to succeed you, one of your own sons, and I will establish his kingdom. He is the one who will build a house for me, and I will establish his throne forever. I will be his father, and he will be my son. I will never take my love away from him, as I took it away from your predecessor. I will set him over my house and my kingdom forever; his throne will be established forever."**(I Chronicles 17:11-14) Two things are to be noted here. **First,** the throne of the son of David is to be established forever.

   In view of what happened just following the death of Solomon, who succeeded David on his earthly throne, and of the subsequent desolation of the commonwealth, the fulfillment of God's promise to David must be found elsewhere than in the perpetuation of an earthly dynasty. The eternal, or everlasting throne of David is to find its fulfillment in the King of Kings. **Secondly**, the promise to David that his seed would sit upon the everlasting throne of His people was unconditional! The promises made to Abraham were conditioned by obedient faith! Among these was the promise of a land in which to dwell. Covenant people are no longer identified with the race of neither Abraham's descendants nor the political commonwealth, which was national Israel. From this point forward, true Israel is the faithful remnant. The lame or bruised are the faithful obedient few. Although they will be bruised in the captivity and dispersion of the nation, God will make of them a remnant. Micah says, "**Jehovah will rule over them.**" (v.7)

4. **The Lord's plan**: **Micah 4:6-7, "In that day," declares the Lord, "I will gather the lame; I will assemble the exiles and those I have brought to grief. (7) "I will make the lame a remnant, those driven away a strong nation. The Lord will rule aver them in Mount Zion from that day and forever."**

   a. Vs. 6-7, "In the day" refers us back to 4:1. **"In the last day the mountain of the Lord's temple will be established."** What Micah is saying it will take place during "last of days" which, we have seen, is the messianic age. Although they will be bruised in the captivity and dispersion of the nation of Israel, God will save a remnant. Through them He will fulfill His covenant promise. The covenant people are no longer identified with descendants or political common wealth, which was national Israel. From this point forward, true Israel is the faithful remnant.

(Note Micah 2:12; **"I will surely gather all of you, O Jacob; I will surely bring together the remnant of Israel. I will bring them together like sheep in a pen, like a flock in its pasture, the place will throng with people."**

(1. Note-"last days"-Rev.22:10-**"Then he told me, "Do not seal up the words of the prophecy of this book, because the time is near . . ."**

5. **FOCUS ON THE MESSIAH-MICAH 5:2-6.**

a. **A PROMIOSED RULER FROM BETHLEHAM —Micah 5:2-5, "But you, Bethlehem Ephrathah, though you are small among the clans of Judah, out of you will come for me one who will be ruler over Israel, whose origins are from of old, from ancient times. (3) Therefore Israel will be abandoned until the time when she who is in labor gives birth and the rest of his brothers return to join the Israelites. (4) He will stand and shepherd his flock in the strength of the Lord, in the majesty of the name of the Lord his God. And they will live securely, for then his greatness will reach to the ends of the earth." (5) And he will be their peace. When the Assyria invades our land and marches through our fortrresses, even eight leaders of men. (6) They will rule the land of Assyria with the sword, the land of Nimrod with drawn sword. He will deliver us from the Assyrian when he invades our land and marches into our borders."**

(1. Verse 2 When the bloodied-handed Herod sent to the rabbis to ask the place of Messiah's birth, he pointed to Bethlehem. (Matt. 2:4-6). It was on the strength of this passage (5:2ff) of Micah's prophecy. No prophecy concerning His coming is more clearer. No predictive Scripture is more

universally agreed upon as to its meaning. Having described the nature of the Messianic age (4:1-13) and having inserted a reminder of the punishment which must come first (5:1). Micah now focuses our attention on the birth and work of the Messiah Himself. Bethlehem! Birthplace of David. Ancient Ephratah of Gentiles, (Gen. 35; 16). The entire race of men have an acute interest in what will happen there. To the Jew first but also to the Greek, there will be born in the city of David a Savior who is Christ the Lord . . . . He who was born there was the lamb of God. The shadow of a cross fell across the manger bed. So firmly fixed was Bethlehem, as the birthplace of the Messiah in the minds of the Jews that Hadrian would allow none of them to live in or near the town.

6. THE GLORIOUS FUTURE OF THE REMNANT. (MICAH 5:7-8; 7:18.)

a. The author concluded his book by reminding himself and his readers about the goodness and uniqueness of their God (cf. Ex. 34:6-7a). Micah's final words of praise show that he had great faith in God's eventual out-working of His plans for His covenant people. Micah's name means, "Who is like Yahweh?" The obvious answer is that no one is like the Lord. The remainder of Micah 7:18-20 describes what He is like. God's acts on behalf of His people prove that He is completely trustworthy and merciful. Micah makes no hesitation in insisting that the demands of God are binding upon the rich and powerful as well as the poor and powerless. He does not preach a 'middle class morality' but eternal ethical right determined by Jehovah.

b. Micah affirmed six things about God:

(1. He pardons the sin and transgression (Micah cf. 1:5; 3:8; 6:7) of the remnant (cf. 2:12; 4:7; 5:7-8) of His inheritance (cf. 7:14).

(2. He does not stay angry forever (cf. Ps. 103:9).

(3. He likes to show mercy; (cf. Micah 7:20).

(4. The Lord will again have compassion, tender and heartfelt compassion "; cf. Ps. 102:13; 103:4, Hosea 14:3; Zech. 10:6) **on** Israel, Micah knew God would do these things because (6) He is **true** (faithful) **to Jacob** and shows **mercy** (cf. v. 18) **to Abraham.**)

(5. God cannot lie; He is true to His Word and loyal to His commitments and His **oath.** Therefore Micah was trusting in God's promises to Abraham (Gen. 12:2-3; 15:18-21), which were confirmed to Jacob (Gen. 28:13-14), that He will bless their descendants.

(6. Israel's peace and prosperity will be realized when the Messiah-King reigns. Christ will exercise justice over His and Israel's opponents and He will extend grace to His own. This promise gave Micah confidence. **(43)**

B. ZEPHANIAH.

1. Throughout the Old Testament the term Yom **WHWH** (day of Jehovah) denotes the time when God's kingdom will be finally complete and free from attack from the outside world or corruption within (cf. Isaiah 2:12. 13:6-9. Ezekiel 13:5, 30:3, Joel 1:15. 2:11, Amos 5:18, and Zephaniah 1:14. To bring this completeness to its fullness four characteristics are described in various contexts, both in the Old and New Testaments: The judgement of

Israel, Judah and the nations of the pre-Christian world;
(2) The deliverance and preservation of the remnants
during and after the captivity; **(3)** The first coming of the
Messiah; and **(4)** The second coming of the Messiah and
His final judgments of all men and nations. Zephaniah
probably wrote in the latter half of Josiah's reign, Josiah
came to the throne at the age of eight, following the death
of his father, Amon, 639 B.C.

2. **THE JUDGEMENT OF GOD: warning of coming
   destruction- Zephaniah CH. 1:1-15.**

   a. **Chap.1:2-3,** The apostle Paul reminds us that,
      **"We know that the whole creation has been
      groaning ... right up to the present time."** (Rom.
      8:22) as a result of man's sin. Peter informs us "The
      day of the Lord will come as a thief; **"The heavens
      will disappear with a roar; ..."** (II Pet. 3:10). Rev.
      21:1 John adds **"Then I saw a new heaven and a
      new earth; ..."** Zephaniah's day of Jehovah to the
      final summing up of all history by God, will not come
      before God's plan to forgive the sin of man through
      His Son and the establishing His Kingdom on earth
      (the Church).

   b. **Universal Judgement Proclaimed, Ch.1:2-3.**

   c. **Judgement of Judah, Ch. 1:4-2:3.**

   d. **GREAT DAY OF JEHOVAH IS NEAR**, Zeph. ch.
      1:14, Here again is the prophetic **"Day of the Lord,"**
      the day in which Jehovah will directly intervene in
      the affairs of man's history in such a way as to reveal
      His judgement and redemption. The Jews, smug in
      their racial identity, were prone to view the day as one
      of extreme gladness for themselves and of extreme
      discomfiture for the Gentiles. Zephaniah's warning is

that the day will be one of anguish for the unfaithful among God's people.

(1. The message addressed to the world of his time is summed up in Zephaniah's repeated use of the term **"day of Jehovah."** Two major ideas are included in this term: (1) the universal judgement of God and (2) the comfort and hope reserved for the remnant.

3. THE JUDGMENT OF GOD IS UNIVERSAL, Zephaniah. Ch. 2:4-15.

a. UNTIL THE DAY . . . Zep. Ch.3:8. Here Zephaniah returns to the theme struck in 1:14. The great Day of Jehovah is again called to mind as the decisive day on which He will gather the nations before Him in wrath.

4. SERVE HIM TOGETHER AS ONE, Zeph. 3:9.

a. Vs. 9 "Then will I purify the lips of the people, that all of them may call on the name of the Lord and serve him shoulder to shoulder.

1.) THE PROMISE OF REDEMPTION, Those who are redeemed not only may, but will serve Him. Jesus promised that the living water of redemption would, in him who drinks, become a fountain, bubbling over to eternal life (cf. John. 4:14). And their service will be with the Lord together with one shoulder. As two oxen pulling against a single yoke, they will serve as one. "In that day" serve Him as one. Here is a glimpse of the unity which characterized the New Testament church, from the day of "Pentecost" forward work together to save the world from sin.

2.) I WILL MAKE THEM A PRAISE AND A NAME . . . V.19-20, In the closing verses the Messianic light of Zephaniah burns brightest . . . . The people righteous and blessed.

3.) SING O DAUGHTER OF ZION . . . V.14.

4.) THE KING OF ISRAEL IS IN THE MIDST.V.15.

5.) LET NOT YOUR HANDS BE SLACK . . . V.16.

6.) I WILL GATHER THEM THAT SORROW . . . V.18. **(44)**

C. ZECHARIAH:

1. **THE PROMISE OF REDEMPTION, Zech. Ch. 3:1-10. and the VISION OF THE HIGH PRIEST.**

   a. As was Haggi, so was Zechariah's purpose the motivation of the people to build the temple. Zechariah's fourth vision continues the growing Messianic crescendo of his prophecy. Here the attention shifts from the city and temple to the high priest. Both the high priest and his fellow priest are presented as a sign to be revealed in the coming of the Branch.

2. **Ch. 3, vs. 1-10 "Then he showed me Joshua the high priest standing before the angel of the Lord, and Satan standing at his right side to accuse him. (2) The Lord said to Satan, "The Lord rebuke you, Satan! The Lord, who has chosen Jerusalem, rebukes you! Is not this man a burning stick snatched from the fire? (3) Now Joshua was dressed in filthy clothes as he stood before the angel (4) The angel said to those**

who were standing before him, "Take off his filthy clothes." Then he said to Joshua, "See I have taken away your sin, and I will put rich garments on you." (5) Then I said, "Put a clean turban on his head," So they put a clean turban on his head and clothed him, while the angel of the Lord stood by. (6) The angel of the Lord gave this charge to Joshua: (7) "This is what the Lord Almighty says: "If you will walk in my ways and keep my requirements, then you will govern my house and have charge of my courts, and I will give you a place among these standing here.

(8) "Listen, O high priest Joshua and your associates seated before you, who are men symbolic of things to come: I am going to bring my servant, the Branch." (9) See, the stone I have set in front of Joshua! There are seven eyes on that one stone, and I will engrave an inscription on it, says the Lord Almighty, and I will remove the sin of this land in a single day. (10) In that day each of you will invite his neighbor to sit under his vine and fig tree, declares the Lord Almighty."

a. Vs. 1-3, Joshua the high priest (Septuagint calls him Jesus), stands before the angel of the Lord as representative of the people.

b. Vs. 4-5, At this point in the vision the angel commands that the filthy garments be removed from Joshua and that they be replaced with rich apparel. A clean turban is to be placed on his head so that he will stand clean before both the angel and Satan. The intent is to show that God is not going to hold the guilt of past sins against his redeemed remnant. Their sins will be forgiven in order that they may get on with His work.

c. Vs. 6-7 Having cleansed the high priest, symbolic of the forgiveness of the people, the angel now addresses him directly. What he says to Joshua is intended to be heard and heeded by the people. He makes two emphatic points.

(1. *First,* their forgiveness was conditional. *If* Joshua will walk in His ways and if he will keep His charge, *then* as high priest he will judge God's house and keep His courts.

(2. V.8, **Second;** Jehovah's angel makes it quite clear that His willingness to forgive His people is related to the fulfillment of a larger purpose and is therefore arbitrary. The entire priesthood, both the high priest and those who sit with him are a sign. The justification of the sins of the people and the ultimate meaning of the priest-hood are to be found in the coming Branch. The Branch is identified as the servant of Jehovah. This is a significant title given the Messiah by both Isaiah and Ezekiel. (Cp. Isaiah 42:1, 49:3, 50:15, 52:13, 53:11, and Ezekiel 34:23,24).

(3. It was primarily the failure of the Jews to see the Messiah in this light that caused their rejection of the Messiah when He came. God was known throughout the earth. Even the people of earth's nations praise them, (cf. Acts 2:47, 5:17, etc.)

(4. Vs. 9-10, To encourage the people toward the building of God's house, the vision now identifies the Messiah as the chief cornerstone of the temple. Upon the stone in the prophet's vision are seven eyes. It is to be engraved by the Master Architect Himself. I Peter 2:4-5 speaks of Jesus much as Zechariah's vision describes Him. He is the living stone chosen of God upon which God's people will build His spiritual house.

(5. (v.9) The Psalmist cried, "Create within me a pure heart O God."(Ps.51:10). Paul wrote ". . . if any man is in Christ, he is a new creature: the old things are passed away, behold they are become new." (II Cor. 5:17).

(6. Zechariah's final message was delivered in 518 B.C.

3. **Zechariah 2:10-13, "Shout and be glad, O Daughter of Zion. For I am coming, and I will live among you," declares the Lord. (11) "Many nations will be joined with the lord in that day and will become my people. I will live among you and you will know that the Lord Almighty has sent me to you. (12) The Lord will inherit Judah as his portion in the Holy Land and will again choose Jerusalem. (13) Be still before the Lord, all mankind, because he has roused himself from his holy dwelling."**

a. Vs. 10-13, In verses 10-13, In the second epilogue the prophet moves from concern with the immediate task of rebuilding which confronted the returnees from Babylon to the future glory of the Messianic kingdom in which many races would come to the Lord. In verse 8, the words "After He has honored me has sent me against the nations," and in verse 9, "Then you that the Lord Almighty has sent me." can only be Messianic in intent.

(1. In verse 10, the Lord promises to dwell personally in the midst of His people. Here is "the promise of the Father" which was fulfilled in the coming of the Holy Spirit to live in the church. Elsewhere God had promised to pour out His Spirit on all flesh. (cf. Acts 1:4, Joel 2:28-ff, Acts 2:16 ff.)

(2. Vs. 11, Paul would write the Galatians and said the purpose of our redemption was "that upon the Gentiles might come the blessing of Abraham in Jesus Christ "that we might receive the promise of the Spirit through faith. (Galatians 3:13-14).

(3. Vs. 12-13, The beginning of Messiah's dwelling in the midst of His people was Jerusalem (Luke 24:47) The heavenly Jerusalem (cp. Heb. 12:22)) had its beginning in the earthly city to be rebuilt by Zechariah's people. The real temple (Heb. 9:8-9), of which the rebuilt temple was a type, a fore-shadowing, was established in the shadow of its material counterpart (Acts 2). So in Messiah's people, God would "yet choose Jerusalem" when men from every nation "come to Mount Zion, and into the city of the loving God, the heavenly Jerusalem . . . to the general assembly and church of the first born who are enrolled in heaven . . . (Heb. 12:22-23). Evidence of this redemptive reconciliation is a "pure Language" (or more accurately, purify the lips of the people). Isaiah, called by God to speak for Him, cried out "I am a man of unclean lips. (Isa. 6:5).

4. **THE PROCLAMATION OF THE MESSIAH —Zechariah 6:9-15.**

a. **Vs 9-15 "The word of the Lord came to me; (10) "Take silver, and gold, from the exiles Heldai, Tobijah and Jedaiah, who have arrived from Babylon. Go the same day to the house of Josiah son of Zephaniah. (11) Take the silver and gold and make a crown, and set it on the head of the high priest, Joshua son of Jehozadak. (12) Tell him this is what the Lord Almighty says: "Here is the man whose name is the Branch, and he will branch out from his place and build the temple of the Lord.**

(13) It is he who will build the temple of the Lord, and he will be clothed with majesty and will sit and rule on his throne. And he will be a priest in his throne. And there will be harmony between the two." (14) The crown will be given to Heldai, Tobijah, Jedaiah and Hen son of Zephaniah as a memorial in the temple of the Lord. (15) Those who are far away will come and help to build the temple of the Lord, and you will know that the Lord Almighty has sent me to you. This will happen if you diligently obey the Lord your God."

(1. Verses 12-15. These verses, the first two of which are the message of Jehovah through Zechariah to Joshua the high priest, from a very definite Messianic prophecy. In the coronation Joshua became **symbolically** the Messiah. The term Branch was previously applied to Joshua in 3:3-9 during the prophet's third vision.

(2. It is stated that Joshua in particular and the accompanying priest in general were together a sign or symbol of "my servant The Branch." Ch. 3:8, Jehovah's angel makes it quite clear that His willingness to forgive His people is related to the fulfillment of a larger purpose and is therefore not arbitrary. The entire priesthood, both the high priest and those who sit with him are a sign. The justification of the sin of the people and the ultimate meaning of the priesthood are to be found in the coming Branch.

Isaiah 11:1-ff. establishes The Branch as a term referring to the Messiah as the promised Seed of David. Isa. 4:2-ff, where the term is used with Messianic meaning for the first time by Isaiah, connects the Branch, with the return of the remnant from captivity. **Christ is** "the Branch," the seed of David. He will be both a priest and a king upon His throne, (cf. Isa. 11:1,2; Rom. 1:3,4; Heb. 4:14-16; I Tim. 6:14-16).

(3. Vs. 13 When the true Branch came, of whom Joshua was only a symbol, He would build the true temple of which the present temple would only be a symbol (cf. Eph. 2:19-22 and Heb. 8:1-2).

5. **ZECHARIAH, ch. 9- THE TRIUMPH OF ZION THROUGH HER MESSIAH.**

a. Theme of chapter nine is the coming of the Messianic King (vs. 9-17). The judgement of God against Israel's traditional enemies is in these opening verses, are to be seen as preparation for that event. Not only God's dealing with these nations as the enemies of His people, but all his dealings in history prior to Messiah's coming were in preparation for it.

(1. The triumph of Zion through her Messiah Zech. Ch. 9.

(2. The judgement against Israel's enemies Zech. Ch. 9:1-8.

b. **The coming of the Zion's King; Zech. 9:9-17.**

c. **Zechariah 9:9-17, "Rejoice greatly, O Daughter of Zion! Shout, Daughter of Jerusalem! See, your king comes to you righteous and having salvation, gentle and riding on a donkey, on a colt, the foal of a donkey." (10) I will take away the chariots from Ephraim and the war-horses from Jerusalem, and the battle bow will be broken. He will proclaim peace to the nations. His rule will extend from sea to sea and from the River to the ends of the earth. (11) As for you, because**

of the blood of my covenant with you, I will free your prisoners from the waterless pit. (12) Return to your fortress, O prisoners of hope; even now I announce that I will restore twice as much to you. (13) I will bend Judah as I bend my bow and fill it with Ephraim. I will rouse your sons, O Zion, against your sons, O Greece, and make you like a warrior's sword. (14) Then the Lord will appear over them; his arrow will flash like lightning. The Sovereign Lord will sound the trumpet; he will march in the storms of the south. (15) And the Lord Almighty will shield them. They will destroy and overcome with slingstones. They will drink and roar, as with wine; they will be full like a bowl used for sprinkling the corners of the altar. (16) The Lord their God will save them on that day as the flock of his people. They will sparkle in his land like jewels in a crown. (17) How attractive and beautiful they will be! Grain will make the young men thrive, and new wine the young women."

(1. Vs. 9-10, Christ will come as a triumphant, but peaceful King (cf. Luke 21:1-5) . . . . Zechariah calls upon the theocratic people, "Doughter of Zion . . . . Daughter of Jerusalem" to rejoice at the coming of her king. (cf. Psalm 2:11) He is not at all what she expected, but He is Messiah.

He is just, a characteristic attributed by the prophets to the Messiah in connection with salvation (cf. Isaiah 45:21; 53:11, Jeremiah 23:5,6). In contrast with Antiochus, whom the Jews mistakenly welcomed as a savior from Egyptian oppression but who came to destroy, the Messiah King will come to save. He is lowly and He comes riding on an ass; not the symbol of humiliation as some have supposed but the symbol of peace, as the horse was a symbol of war. This verse finds its literal fulfillment in Jesus' final entry into Jerusalem. (cp. Matt. 21:4-5).

(2. Vs. 11-17, With the words, "as for you also," Zechariah turns to the coming deliverance from Greek oppression. It will be because of the covenant that the people will be rescued from the threat of complete extinction by Hellenization.

6. **ISRAEL RESTORED IN-Zechariah Chap. 10:**

a. **The Lord will care for Judah, Ch.10:1-12.**

b. In chapter nine, verses nine through ten, Zechariah predicts the coming of Messiah. In 9:11-17, and the victorious struggle with the Greeks, which would precede His actual coming. In chapter ten Zion triumphant through the Messiah.

c. **vs. 1 "Ask the Lord for rain in the springtime; It is the Lord who makes the storm clouds. He gives showers of rain to men, and plants of the field to everyone."**

(1. v.1- The key to this chapter seems to be "in the time of the latter rain." To understand the symbolism here, we must know something of the climate of the holy land. During summer it almost literally never rains. From May first, Through October fifteenth, one can almost guarantee no rain will fall. The rainy season, from October to May, comes in three parts. They are known as the first or former rains, the winter rains, and the latter rains. The former are the light rains of October and the early days of November.

These moisten the soil after the summer drought and allow the planting of winter grain. The heaviest rains are the winter rains, which fall during December, January and February. The bulk of the water in the land comes from these rains. Most vital to the completion of the harvest are the **latter rains**. These perfect the fruit and grain just prior to harvest, and so are most welcome and celebrated of all (cf. Joel 2:21-24). In a land where water is always in such critical supply as in Palestine, it is not surprising that rain should be a favorite symbol of divine blessing (cf. Isaiah 44:3-4; Hosea 6:3 Psalms 72:6). By "rain in the time of the later rain," Zechariah means God's blessing at the critical point in the history of His people when the fruit of His purpose was nearly ripe for harvest. The coming of the Messiah would usher in the fulfillment of God's purpose in Israel. **(45)**

7. Ch. 10:3-4, **"My anger burns against the shepherds, and I will punish the leaders; for the Lord Almighty will care for his flock, the house of Judah, and make them like a proud horse in battle. (4) From Judah will come the cornerstone, from him the tent peg, from him the battle bow, from him every ruler."**

   a. Vs. 3, The shepherds are the spiritual leaders of the people, the male goats, the civil leaders. Previously those who held these positions had led the people after false gods. God's anger is kindled against such leadership. He will not allow it to go unpunished. Jehovah has personally visited His flock. They are no longer to be victimized by such leadership. Here we again see Zechariah's messianic insight. In the coming of the Messiah, Jehovah visited His flock, the house of Judah.

   b. Vs. 4, The Jews were no longer to be subject to foreign rule. "From him," ie. From Judah, shall come its ruler. The Maccabean deliverers from Aniochus Epiphanes fulfilled the primary meaning of this prophetic promise, but it looks forward to the Messiah.

   The figure of the corner-stone is one of the best known of those applied to the Christ in the New Testament. Jesus applied it to Himself, (cf. Matt. 21:42, Mark 12:10, Luke

20:17). Peter applied it to Him (Act. 4:11, I Peter 2:7) as did Paul (Eph. 2:20).

8. A PARABLE OF SHEPHERDS Zechariah ch. 11.

a. Between the time Zechariah and the establishment of the Jewish people as described in the last section, there was to be another period during which they will feel the wrath of Jehovah. The time of the fulfillment of this prediction is fixed beyond question by verses twelve and thirteen. The verses are applied very literally to the betrayal of Jesus in (Matt. 26:5, 27:9-10).

b. **The Shepherd pays the price, Ch. 11:12-14.**

c. **Chap. 11:12-14 "I told them, "If you think it best, give me my pay; but if not, keep it." So they paid me thirty pieces of silver. (13) And the Lord said to me, "Throw it to the potter," the handsome price at which they priced me! So I took the thirty pieces of silver and threw them in the house of the Lord to the potter." (14) Then I broke my second staff called Union, breaking the brotherhood between Judah and Israel."**

   (1. The final act of unfaithfulness came when the Good Shepherd appealed to the Jews for His hire, for that which was rightly His in payment for all he had done for them. Christ will be sold for thirty pieces of silver, (Matt. 26:14-16; 47-50; 27:3-10) Verses 12-14. Even without the covenant, His care, **protection** and even His choosing the Jewish people above the other races of the world should have entitled Him to their acceptance and undying allegiance. Instead they betrayed Him, and sold Him for the price of an injured slave. Thirty pieces of silver (about $25) was the amount fixed by law in compensation for the injury of another's slave. (cp. Exodus 21:32).

The accuracy of Zechariah's prophecy is seen in the fulfillment of it in the detailed disposal of the money paid Judas. *"cast unto the potter"* (Matt. 27:9) quotes the prophecy of Jeremiah 1:18-19 that mentions this fact also. And the money returned by Judas prior to his suicide was used to purchase a potter field. (Acts 1:18-19 mentions Judas reward)

9. **ZECHARIAH Ch.12-13; "IN THE FIRST DAY".**

a. Chapter 12,13 and 14 actually compose a single unit of thought, which climaxes Zechariah's prophecy in a blaze of apocalyptic eschatology, some of which is nearly impossible to understand clearly. The key to these final chapters is found in the phrase **"in the day"** which is repeated no less than sixteen times throughout the passage. The unit of thought is expressed in regard to **two "days"**, which from Zechariah's point of view remained in the future. The first day and its happening comprise 12:3-13:7 and prefigures the Messianic age. The final day of the Lord is described in the final chapter, 14:21. We note there four characteristics of **"that day"** **(1)** the judgement of Israel, Judah and the nations of the pre-Christian world. **(2)** The deliverance and preservation of the remnant during and after the captivity, **(3)** the first coming of the Messiah and **(4)** the second coming of the Messiah and His final judgement of all men and nations. To understand Zechariah's **"in that day"** we must be alert to all four elements.

9. **MOURNING FOR THE ONE THEY PIERCED- Zechariah Ch. 12:9-14-13:1.**

a. **On that day-Ch. 12:9-14.**

b. **Chap. 12:9-14 "On that day I will set out to destroy all the nations that attack Jerusalem. (10) And I will pour out on the house of David and the inhabitants of**

Jerusalem a spirit of grace and supplication. They will look on me, the one they have pierced, and they will mourn for him as one mourns for an only child, and grieve bitterly for him as one grieves for a firstborn son. 11) On that day the weeping in Jerusalem will be great, like the weeping of Hadad Rimmon in the plain of Megiddo.

(12) The land will mourn, each clan by itself, with their wives by themselves; the clan of the house of David and their wives, the clan of the house of Nathan and their wives, (13) the clan of the house of Levi and their wives, the clan Shimei and their wives, (14) and all the rest of the clans and their wives."

(1. V.9-The few followers of Jesus in the early days of the church soon found themselves the object of the most savage religious persecution ever, to that time, raised against a people. Peter described the persecution in words borrowed from Zechariah 13:9, in I Peter 1:6,7.

(2. Vs.10, It is this verse which fixes "On that day" in this section as the Messianic age.

(3. Vs.11-14- The apostle John sees in Jesus' death the fulfillment of this verse. (cf. John 19:34-37) John also recalls this verse in connection with the second coming. (cf. Revelation 1:7) Some have seen in the mourning for Him whom they have pierced a prediction that the Jews will be converted to Christ. This cannot, of course, be ruled out, **(because the first converts to Christ were Jews.)** Paul speaks of the possibility that the Jews who rejected Jesus may be grafted into God's true Israel. This however, is definitely conditioned upon **". . . if they continue not in their unbelief." (Rom. 11:17-24).**

c. **Zech. 13:1-"On that day a fountain will be opened to the house of David and the inhabitants of Jerusalem, to cleanse them from sin and impurity."**

(1. **vs. 13:1** The fountain (Christ) will be opened for sin and cleansing (cf. John 1:29; Matt. 26:28). In connection with the mourning over Him whom they pierced, a fountain is to be opened for sin and uncleanness. Sin is transgression against the law of God, (I John 3:4). Uncleanness is that condition of one's soul, which makes him unfit for the presence of God. The death of David's Branch (cp. 3:8 and 6:12), who is seen here in the hour of His death (pierced) provides the fountain for sin and uncleanness. Jesus' understanding of the Old Testament was that the Christ should suffer, and rise again the third day. When this has been done, repentance and remission of sin is to be preached in His name. (cf. Luke 24:44-47).

10. **The second day. Ch. 14**

a. If overall understanding of Zechariah to this point is correct chapter fourteen, deals almost exclusively with eschatology. Eschatology may be defined simply as the study of the last things, or times. Most commentators agree that this is the subject matter of the present chapter. (14) However, unanimity of opinion, concerning Zechariah's last chapter ends with this agreement. Rabid pre-millenialists have a field day here, as they do with the other apocalyptic writings of the Bible, because of the apocalyptic nature of the works itself. They see here the proof of their contention that Jesus plans, upon His second coming to establish an earthly kingdom which will stand for a thousand years, and in which the Jews, with Him as king, will rule the world, and in general do what Jesus refused to do the first time He came to earth. They also claim the Jews will do what the church has failed to do, namely convert the world to Jehovah and Christ If that is the case, why did Jesus say to His disciples, "All authority in heaven and on earth has been given to me. Therefore go and make disciples of all nations, baptizing them in the name of the Father and of the Son and of the Holy Spirit, and teaching them to obey every thing I have commanded you . . ." And Acts 2:38,-"Peter replied, "Repent and be baptized, every one of you, in the name of Jesus Christ for the forgiveness of our sins. And you will receive the gift of the Holy Spirit." When you have taken on Christ in baptism, you have been converted to Jehovah (God) and Christ. So the church has fulfilled its commission to Jesus' commandment in Matthew 28!

    b. Gal. 3:26-29-**"You are all sons of God through faith in Christ Jesus, for all of you who were baptized into Christ have clothed yourselves with Christ. There is neither Jew nor Greek, slave nor free, male nor female, for you are all one in Christ Jesus, If you belong to Christ, then you are Abraham's seed, and heirs according to the promise." (46)**

D. MALACHI; Messenger of Jehovah.

    a. **THE COMING DAY OF THE LORD-Malachi 2:17-3:6.**

    b. **Ch.3:1 " See I will send my messenger, who will prepare the way before me"** . . . This points to the forerunner of the Messiah. The next word from Jehovah to His people is John the Baptist preaching. (John 1:6-9)

        (1. Ch. 3:1, <u>**"See, I will send my messenger, who will prepare the way before me. Then suddenly the Lord you are seeking will come to his temple; the messenger of the covenant, whom you desire, will come," says the Lord Almighty."**</u>

(a. **Here God answered their question.** "Where is the God of justice." (ch.2;17) Suddenly the Lord will appear in the temple heralded by His forerunner. Isaiah had made a similar prediction. (Isa. 40:3-5) The New Testament applies Malachi's prophecy to John the Baptist. (cf. Matt. 3:3, 11:10; Mark 1:2-3; Luke 1:76, 7:26-27; John 1:23. **"The messenger of the Covenant,"** What better description could there have been for Jesus, whose coming was the very heart of God's promise to His people!

(b. **Note** that the writer of Hebrews will introduce the comparison of the Old and New Covenants with the argument for the superiority of the New based on the superiority of the Son over the prophets, angels and Moses, who were the messengers of the Old. (cf. Heb. 1:1-24)

12. The coming day of the Lord, "If the people will return in devotion to God He will yet bless them. Malachi 3:6-12.

a. <u>Ch. 3:6-12, "I the Lord do not change. So you, O descendants of Jacob, are not destroyed. (7) Ever since the time of your forefathers you have turned away from my decrees and have not kept them. Return to me, and I will return to you, "says the Lord Almighty." But you ask, "How are we to return? (8) "Will a man rob God? Yet you rob me. "But you ask, 'How do we rob you?' "In tithes and offerings. (9) You are under a curse, the whole nation of you, because you are robbing me. (10) Bring the whole tithe into the storehouse, that there may be food in my house. Test me in this," says the Lord Almighty, "and see if I will not throw open the floodgates of heaven and pour out so much blessing that you will not have room enough for it.</u>

(11) I will prevent pests from devouring your crops, and the vines in your fields will not cast their fruit," says the Lord Almighty. (12) "Then all the nations will call you blessed, for yours will be a delightful land," says the Lord Almighty.

(1. **vs.6,** It is a tragic error to assume that, because God has not smitten the wicked, He has changed from a God of justice to one of easy-going tolerance. Malachi points out to his readers that God's unchanging nature is the only reason they were not themselves long since wiped out! Paul points out in Romans eleven (cf. v.29) that God's mercy toward even the covenant people finds its source in His unfailing faithfulness to His own covenant.

(2. **vs. 7,** When Stephen stood before the council and accused them, "You stiff-necked and uncircumcised in heart and ears . . . as your fathers did, so do you," (Acts 7:51) he was in good company. Malachi here levels the same charge against his readers. Just as their ancestors had turned aside from God's ordinances to worship Baal, these are turning aside in making a mockery of the same ordinances. The entreaty of God to such people to return to Him is frequently met today as in Malachi's time (v.7) with a blank face and feigned innocence expressed in "wherein shall we return?" (c) **vs. 8-12,** Malachi's answer to this sham is "will a man rob God?" When their response was again an assumed innocence expressed in, "where have we robbed you," the prophet goes directly to the heart of the matter . . . **"In tithes and offerings."** That they could answer in such false righteousness after what the prophet has written in the preceding chapters about their unholy sacrifices is amazing.

13. When the day comes, true Worshippers will be spared.-Malachi 3:16-17

    a. v.17; "They shall be Mine" It is those who fear Jehovah and think on His name who are His people. There is no preference made to religion or racial origin. Peter points out in Romans eleven (cf. v29) that God's mercy toward even the covenant people finds its source in His unfailing faithfulness to His own covenant. Peter speaks to the same fatal fallacy when he writes,

    b. **(2 Pet. 3:9). "The Lord is not slow in keeping his promise, as some understand slowness. He is patient with you, not wanting anyone to perish, but everyone to come to repentance."**

    c. **The day of Justice-Malachi 2:17, <u>"You have wearied the Lord with, "How have we wearied him? You ask. By saying, "all who do evil are good in the eyes of the Lord, and he is pleased with them" or." Where is the God of Justice?</u>**

14. BEHOLD, THE DAY COMING, Malachi 4:1-3.

    a. **Ch.4:1, <u>"Surely the day is coming; it will burn like a furnace. All the arrogant and every evildoer will be stubble, and that day that is coming will set them on fire," says the Lord Almighty. "Not a root or a branch will be left to them"</u>**

        (1. Note (Dan. 7;9-10). Malachi promises that those that feel this final fire will be without hope of springing again to life. They will be without branch or root. (See Amos 2:9)

        (2. 1 Thess. 4:13-18.

b. **4:2-3 "But for you who revere my name, the sun of righteousness will rise with healing in its wings. And you will go out and leap like calves released from the stall. (3) Then you will trample down the wicked; they will be ashes under the soles of your feet on the day when I do these things," says the Lord Almighty.**

(1. Verse 3, When this day comes, and the wicked are punished by fire while God's people are freed from all care, the question of 3:15 will finally be answered. Jesus' rehearsal of the fate of the rich man and Lazarus is a fine illustration of this truth (cf. Luke 16:19ff.) Malachi's promise of Elijah's coming is fulfilled in the ministry of John the Baptist. Jesus began where Malachi left off and being aware continued the work of the prophets. His ministry is understood only in light of God's plan to redeem the entire world through a people prepared as the instrument of divine worldwide purpose. (cf. Luke 24:44-47 and Ephesians 1:23) **(47)**

15. THE GENEALOGY AND BIRTH OF JESUS-Matt. 1:1-2:9.

a. v. 17, <u>**"Thus there were fourteen generation in all from Abraham to David, fourteen generations from David to the exile to Babylon, and fourteen from the exile to the Christ."**</u>

b. <u>**2:9, "After they had heard the king, they went on their way, and the star they had seen in the east went ahead of them until it stopped over the place where the child was.**</u>

16. THE FULFILLMENT OF THE PROPOHECY; THE DEATH, BURIAL AND RESURRECTION OF JESUS-Matt. 27:45-28:5.

   a. 27:46, "About the ninth hour Jesus cried out in a loud voice, *ELOI, ELOI, LAMA SABACHT HANI?" which means, MY GOD, MY GOD, WHY HAVE YOU FORSAKEN ME?" .... v :50, And when Jesus had cried out again in a loud voice, he gave up his spirit."*

   b. 28:5, "The angel said to the women, "Do not be afraid, for I know that you are looking for Jesus, who was crucified. He is not here He has risen, just as he said . . ."

17. Caring passages—Birth of Jesus Luke 2:1-40-The crucifixion and resurrection of Jesus, John 19:16b-21:25.

BIBLIOGRAPHY

I. Bible History Old Testament, By Alfred Edershen. William B. Eerdmans Pub. Co. Grand Rapids Fifth Printing. November 1980.p.13.

II. LOGOS Bible Software, Libronix Digital Library System (Bible Knowledge Commentary.) Ephesians by HAPO LD W. HOEHN ER.

III. ISAIAH:1 & 11; 111, Paul T. Butler, College Press, Joplin, Missouri, Copyright; 1975; 1975.

IV. EZEKIEL: James E. Smith, College Press, Joplin, Missouri, Copyright Third Printing 1989,

V. MINOR PROPHETS—A Study of Micah through Malachi by Clinton R. Gill. College Press, Joplin, Missouri. Copyright 1971.

VI. BIBLIOGRAPHY BY PUBLISHER AND AUTHOR.

  1. BIBLE HISTORY OLD TESTAMENT; 1.

  2. LIBRONIX DIGITAL; 4, ibid,5, 6, 7, 8, 11, 12, 13, 14, 15, 17,19,20, 21,22, 24, 25, 29, 33, 36,43.

  3. COLLEGE PRESS: ISAIAH 1& 11; 2, ibid,3, 9, 10, 16, 18,23,26, 27, 28, 30, 31, 32, 34,35,37.

4. COLLEGE PRESS: EZEKIEL; 38.ibid,39.

5. COLLEGE PRESS; MINER PROPHETS 11:40, ibid, 41, 42,44,45,46,47.

VII. This author would recommend that anyone who is a student of God's Word, to purchase the College Press commentary for further study.

SPECIAL STUDY

By
LOGOS BIBLE SOFTWARE, LIBRONIX
DIGITAL LIBRARY

There is a knowledge that must be known by people of the world, so Paul identifies himself as an apostle, called by the will of God, vs.1. Then he explains the magnitude of God's plan. Eph. 1:3-10. Verses 3-14 are dominated by and structured around God's action, which is all directed "to the praise of his glory" (vss. 5,12,14). This phrase culminates sections, which center receptively on the activity of God, Christ, and the Holy Spirit. Paul introduces the explanation of the spiritual blessing. God elected us, Christians, and were chosen before the creation, the foundation of the world, indicating that 'God's purpose in Christ has been his plan from the beginning (cf. Peter 1:20). Paul now uses the sacrificial terminology of the Old Testament, stating that it is 'God's desire to present the church to himself holy and blameless before him (see Eph. 5; 27, Col. 1:22; Phil. 2:15; Deut. 32:5).

A. **Paul now explains the mystery that has been hidden and now has been reviled to Paul. Ephesians 2:19. Consequently you,** that is, Gentile believers, **are no longer (Foreigners and Strangers (K.J.V.)** (cf. v. 12) **and (aliens N.I.V.).** Believing Gentiles become **fellow citizens with God's people and members of God's household.** They become a part of the company of the redeemed of all ages beginning with Adam. However, this does not mean that the church inherits the blessings promised to Israel. There are three reasons for this: (1) In the context Paul was discussing the "one new man" (v. 15), the "one body" (v. 16). This does not mean that Gentiles are incorporated into Israel but that believing Jews and Gentiles are incorporated into one new humanity'. **The Church** (2) Paul specifically stated that Gentiles are incorporated "with God's people" and are in "God's household" (v. 19); he did not use the word "Israel." If Paul meant that the church became "Israel," he would have named both groups, as he did in verse 11. Paul explained that this new relationship is "built on the foundation of the apostles and prophets with Christ Jesus Himself as the chief Cornerstone" (v. 20). This began on the day of Pentecost, not in the Old Testament. True, Gentile believers become a part of the redeemed of all ages (v. 19). But their being incorporated with Jewish believers into the "one new man" distinctly began when the church came into being at Pentecost. Paul indicates that what has been revealed has come by the Spirit of God, not by human attainment.

B. **Eph. 3:5,6 Paul then revealed the time when the mystery was disclosed.** The mystery **was not made known to men in other generations as it has been revealed to him. Even the angels desired to know (1 Peter 1:12).** The manifold wisdom of God" (which is the mystery) is "now" to be made known to the heavenly hosts. If the heavenly hosts did not know of the mystery in the Old Testament, how would people have found out about it? Since the heavenly hosts learned of the mystery through the church (which did not exist before Pentecost) certainly people in the Old Testament did not know. (5) "Revealed" means "to uncover or unveil" something that has previously been completely covered or hidden. Therefore it would be wrong to say the mystery was *partially* uncovered in the Old Testament. This mystery was revealed **by the Spirit** (cf. Eph. 2:22), and its recipients were **God's holy apostles and prophets** (cf. 2:20; 4:11). Verse 17 begins in with the Greek word "and" (untranslated in the niv). This links verse 17 with verse 14. Not only is Christ "our peace" (v. 14), but **He** also **preached peace.** When did Christ do this? Certainly this refers to the preaching of peace by the apostles rather than Christ Himself because Christ preached almost entirely to Jews (Matt. 10:5-6; 15:24-27). (Christ said in Matt. 10:34, "Do not suppose that I have come to bring peace to the earth. I did not come to bring peace, but a sword, . . ." cf. Luke 12:51; John 14:27.) Also the peace that was preached was on the basis of Christ's death rather than during His life on earth. **Peace** is supplied both **to** those **who were far away** (cf. Eph. 2:13), that is, Gentiles (who were without Christ and alienated from Israel and her covenants, v. 12) and **to those who were near,** namely, Jews (who have "the covenants of the promise," v. 12). As a result of this message of peace both Jewish and Gentile believers **have access to** God **the Father by one Spirit** (cf. 1 Cor. 12:13). Access can mean "introduction" in the sense that Christ *is* a believer's "introduction" to the Father. But it seems better to understand that Christ *gives* believers access. The Greek word for access **(prosagōgēn, "approach")** is used elsewhere in the New Testament only in Romans 5:2 and Ephesians 3:12. As so often in this book the work of the Trinity is seen. Here believers have access to God the Father through the Holy Spirit because of Christ's death on the cross. In four ways in 2:14-18 Paul emphasized that the two (Jew and Gentile) have been united. (1) "The two" are made *"one"* (v. 14), (2) *"one* new man" is created "out of the two" (v. 15), (3) "in this *one* body . . . both" are reconciled (v. 16), and (4) "both" have access . . . by *one* Spirit (v. 18). Nothing could be clearer than the fact that this new union replaces hatred. So the two (Jews) and (Gentiles) are now one in Christ, the now Israel the Church